Gin

THE ULTIMATE
COMPANION

Gin

THE ULTIMATE COMPANION

Ian Buxton

BIRLINN

First published in 2021 by
Birlinn Limited
West Newington House
10 Newington Road
Edinburgh
EH9 1QS
www.birlinn.co.uk

ISBN: 978 1 78027 753 0

British Library Cataloguing-in-Publication Data
A catalogue record for this book is available from the British Library

Designed and typeset by Teresa Monachino
Printed and bound by PNB, Latvia

CONTENTS

INTRODUCTION

Gin's Still Crazy

Well, what about gin! Not so many years ago, gin was on the skids. Drinkers were getting older and older, even leading brands were value engineering their product (37.5% Gordon's – really?), and the big marketing budgets had been diverted to vodka and white rum, which was where the cool kids were to be found. Gin was a career graveyard and it was all too apparent that no one really cared. Certainly no one under fifty would be seen dead drinking it.

Then, out of the blue, along came Bombay Sapphire (1986), followed in 1999 by Hendrick's. They changed everything. Slowly, but with increasing enthusiasm, new consumers took to them: partly led by some forward-thinking bartenders – notably the late Dick Bradsell; partly because they just tasted better – fresh, new, different; and partly because the drinks industry woke up to the fact that you didn't have to cut quality and prices to sell worthwhile volumes. The 'premiumisation' of gin had begun, though gin was still in the hands of the big producers and innovation was limited by a strict adherence to the conventionally approved juniper-dominated style (apart from the iconoclastic incomers mentioned above). But change was in the wind.

It took a change in the law controlling distilling, around 2007, to set the scene for the seismic changes that brought us to today, where there are more gins than anyone can count. Indeed, scarcely a day goes by without an established brand offering a fresh take on their established styles or, more likely, a new boutique distillery opening its doors – where gin is *de rigueur* and convention challenged with a degree of gleeful abandon that has probably never before been seen in the drinks industry. Almost anything goes, and there seems little sign of things slowing down. In fact, gin seems to be taking over the world, with new small distilleries opening up at a furious pace and gin, very tasty gin, being produced where it had never previously featured. I was going to mention Japan here (well, I just have) but, as I was writing, someone emailed me about a new gin produced in Botswana. Now, that is unexpected.

However, before we dive into the particular madness of our twenty-first-century Gin Craze a little bit of history is probably called for.

A Little Bit of History

According to the Middlesex magistrates, gin was 'the principal cause of all the vice and debauchery committed among the inferior sort of people'. Clearly, those gentlemen took a robust and not very politically correct view of those making an involuntary and no doubt unwelcome visit to their court in 1721 …

So, things were pretty over-excited in Georgian England, which for most of the early eighteenth century was in the grip of a binge-drinking frenzy we've come to know as the Gin Craze. Daniel Defoe put up a pretty robust defence of the industry though:

> As to the excesses and intemperances of the People, and their drinking immoderate Quantities of Malt Spirits, the Distillers are not concern'd in it at all; their Business is to prepare a Spirit wholesome and good. If the People will destroy themselves by their own Excesses, and make that Poison, which is otherwise an Antidote; 'tis the Magistrates' Business to help that, not the Distillers.

> – *The Case of the Distillers* (London, 1726)

Mind you, Defoe had been well paid for that piece of enthusiastic spin-doctoring and was as liable to take the side of the moral majority as he was to defend the distilling industry, which, incidentally and apart from some pious sermonising about 'using our products responsibly', hasn't to this day got much further than 'don't blame us if people get off their face on our products'.

Gin's history begins … well, no one can quite agree. According to some commentators, not least the ever reliable Wikipedia (so it must be true), the Dutch physician Franciscus Sylvius is to be credited with the invention of gin in the mid-seventeenth century.

But 'Dutch courage' can be dated to 1585 when English troops supported the Dutch army in their war with the Spanish, and there are written references to 'genever' as early as the thirteenth century.

I'm not convinced that it matters. Various nations make various claims for the ancient origins of their national drink: the Scots date whisky to 1494, the Poles claim 1174 for vodka, and the French place Armagnac ahead of cognac with references to 1411. So, the English were late to the game with gin, probably sometime in the early seventeenth century. The Worshipful Company of Distillers, Defoe's patron, received their royal warrant in 1638, but the first 'distillers' were actually surgeons, much to the displeasure of the apothecaries who took exception to these upstarts and objected to the dilution of their jealously guarded privileges.

The first attempts at gin were an effort to replicate the genever enjoyed by English troops during their long campaigns in Holland during the Thirty Years' War (1618–48), but it took the arrival of King William III, or William of Orange as he is better known, in the Glorious Revolution of 1688 for gin to raise its game. And raise it, it did, helped by laws which promoted distilling in England (and, not entirely coincidentally, the sale of grain – which suited the landed interest then dominant in Parliament very nicely indeed).

Soon sales of gin exceeded that of the more expensive beer; little wonder when anyone could start distilling by giving ten days' public notice. To the alarm of the genteel and the ruling classes, production soared, and in 1729 a licensing system for distillers and publicans was introduced and duty charged. Things got worse: illicitly distilled 'gin' prospered at the expense of legitimate traders, and soon it was estimated that in certain parts of London one private house in four was selling some form of spirits. Regionally, the situation was little better and an epidemic of alcohol dependency was taking hold of the poorer parts of the nation.

A further attempt at legislation, the Gin Act of September 1736, merely exacerbated the situation by attempting to restrict retailers and greatly raise the selling price. Though opposed by, among others, Prime Minister Sir Robert Walpole and Dr Samuel Johnson, the law was passed – and then routinely ignored. Only two of the infamous £50 distilling licences (equivalent to around £750,000 today) were taken out, while production is thought to have increased by around half. Rioting followed the passing of the Act, though street riots were not infrequent during this period: 1736 saw the Porteous Riots of April and September in Edinburgh, and in East London in July of that year there were riots against the cheap labour of Irish immigrants. A number of pamphlets arguing for and against the measure were issued, some with extravagant titles such as 'An Elegy on the much-lamented death of the most excellent, the most truly beloved, and universally admired Lady

Madam Geneva'. The lady also appeared in a famous print, *The Funeral Procession of Madam Geneva. Sepr. 29. 1736.*

Social problems associated with excessive drinking and the public consumption of spirits, such as crime and prostitution, continued, and Parliament, accepting that the 1736 Act was unworkable, returned to the subject in 1742/43. The earlier legislation was abolished and a fairer system of licensing and taxation was introduced, partly following lobbying from the distilling industry. This was further refined in 1747, but the problems remained.

By 1751, the novelist and magistrate Henry Fielding, active in the suppression of the gin trade, attributed to it 'the late [i.e. *recent*] increase in robbers' and may have worked with, or influenced, his friend William Hogarth whose engravings *Gin Lane* and *Beer Street* dramatically illustrate the scourge of excessive gin drinking in graphic scenes of misery, vice, degradation and death. Hogarth contrasts the squalor resulting from gin consumption with the robust health of the beer drinker, illustrating a street scene where only the pawnbroker's business appears to be suffering. Moralistic verses by the Reverend James Townley appear beneath both images, his poem on gin beginning:

Gin cursed Fiend, with Fury fraught,
Makes human Race a Prey,
It enters by a deadly Draught,
And steals our Life away.

But by 1757 the Gin Craze had subsided. In part this was due to the 1751 legislation which required licensees to trade from premises rented for at least £10 a year and thus tended to favour larger, better-quality producers. Historians also point to population growth, poor harvests and the consequent reduction in wages and higher food prices as contributory factors. Gin production simply became less profitable, and so the trade declined until the next boom in Victorian times – and the arrival of the gin palace.

These lavish and alluring premises flourished from the late 1820s and provided a vivid contrast to the squalid dram shops that preceded them. Large, dramatically lit and filled with cut glass and mirrors, they were originally designed for fast service, where the patron was intended to consume his or her drink standing up and then leave to make way

By 1802 gin had fallen in popularity. Here, Prime Minister Viscount Sidmouth (left) tries to convince John Bull of the merits of 'Genuine Royal Gin'. His wife Hibernia (Ireland) presses the claims of whiskey while John prefers 'good Bread and Beer'.

for the next customer. Their influence on pub design was profound and they made a notable impact on the novelist Charles Dickens who describes them at length in the *Evening Chronicle* of 19 February 1835:

All is light and brilliancy. The hum of many voices issues from that splendid gin-shop which forms the commencement of the two streets opposite; and the gay building with the fantastically ornamented parapet, the illuminated clock, the plate-glass windows surrounded by stucco rosettes, and its profusion of gas-lights in richly gilt burners, is perfectly dazzling when contrasted with the darkness and dirt we have just left. The interior is even gayer than the exterior. A bar of French-polished mahogany, elegantly carved, extends the whole width of the place; and there are two side-aisles of great casks, painted green and gold, enclosed within a light brass rail, and bearing such inscriptions, as 'Old Tom, 549'; 'Young Tom, 360'; 'Samson, 1421' – the figures agreeing, we presume, with 'gallons', understood. Beyond the bar is a lofty and spacious saloon, full of the same enticing vessels, with a gallery running round it, equally well furnished. On the counter, in addition to the usual spirit apparatus, are two or three little baskets of cakes and biscuits, which are carefully secured at top with wicker-work, to prevent their contents being unlawfully abstracted. Behind it, are two showily dressed damsels with large necklaces, dispensing the spirits and 'compounds'. They are assisted by the ostensible proprietor of the concern, a stout, coarse fellow in a fur cap, put on very much on one side to give him a knowing air, and to display his sandy whiskers to the best advantage.

In his essay, Dickens is highly critical of the prevailing social conditions of the poorer working classes and the unemployed but very well aware of the appeal of the gin palace. He concludes:

> Gin-drinking is a great vice in England, but wretchedness and dirt are a greater; and until you improve the homes of the poor, or persuade a half-famished wretch not to seek relief in the temporary oblivion of his own misery, with the pittance which, divided among his family, would furnish a morsel of bread for each, gin-shops will increase in number and splendour.

Later, in *The Life and Adventures of Martin Chuzzlewit* (1844) we meet the sublime Sairey Gamp: 'The face of Mrs Gamp – the nose in particular – was somewhat red and swollen, and it was difficult to enjoy her society without becoming conscious of a smell of spirits.'

Dickens' vivid stereotype lingered for some time. However, as British imperial power expanded, to become at its zenith the empire on which the sun never set, the medicinal use of quinine to prevent malaria became more widespread. French scientists had extracted quinine from the bark of the cinchona tree in 1817, but the taste was bitter and unpalatable. Soon though, British officers in India, no doubt imbued with patriotic fervour and keen to support domestic industry while helping their medicine go down, hit on the idea of combining it with soda water, sugar, lime and gin.

Thus, as early as 1825 we see the forerunner of the gin and tonic, and gin beginning to move upmarket. Bottles of sweetened quinine water soon appeared and carbonated tonic water was introduced towards the end of the nineteenth century. Meanwhile Johann Schweppe had founded his eponymous business in Vienna in 1783 (he moved to London nine years later).

Some of the greatest names in gin date from this period, or just earlier. Greenall's was founded in 1761, Gordon's in 1769, and Plymouth in 1793, but with the advent of Tanqueray (1830) and Beefeater (1860s, but building on a firm established some forty years earlier) branding and marketing came to the fore.

Having swept round the British Empire, gin enjoyed its next moment of fame and popularity during the cocktail boom of the Roaring Twenties. Again, it had successfully moved upmarket and was fashionable, acceptable in society, and had crossed the Atlantic to conquer America. The advent of Prohibition does not appear to have significantly dented its appeal, with the 'bathtub gin' of legend (and, all too often, fact) lending it an edgy glamour and racy charm. The lure of the speakeasy and the blandishments of the bootlegger are an uncomfortable echo of England's Gin Craze.

As late as 1942, Rick (Humphrey Bogart) describes his bar in *Casablanca* as a 'gin joint' – something clandestine, outside the law and carrying the fascination of forbidden fruit. By the 1950s, however, it had shaken off this raffish clothing and become respectable: now it was something served in golf clubs to the middle-aged and middle-class. Long-established brands began to fail, and old favourites such as Lemon Gin, Orange Gin and Old Tom fell away one by one. Little wonder that within a few short years vodka and white rum would overtake it and gin's slow decline would accelerate. But that was dramatically reversed with the arrival of brands such as Bombay Sapphire and Hendrick's.

Which brings us almost to the present day, where we find an excitement and energy about gin that has not been seen for more than a hundred years. Goodness knows how many brands are available worldwide, with more and more daily arrivals.

How Gin Is Made

This is the briefest of descriptions because a number of books and many websites deal with the technical description in great depth and with considerable expertise. Many of the brand entries also expand on aspects of production.

Gin is made from high-strength pure distilled spirit, normally from grain or molasses, which is selected for its clean neutral flavour. Grape-based spirit and, occasionally, beetroot may also be used, though neutral grain spirit (NGS) predominates. In the case of London Dry gin, the best-known style, the neutral spirit is redistilled in the presence of botanicals to give the resultant gin its flavour. Following distillation, nothing is permitted to be added other than neutral alcohol, water to reduce the spirit to bottling strength, and a tiny amount of sugar. 'London' defines the style, and production may take place anywhere: it does not indicate geographical origin.

Starting with juniper, which must be its main or characteristic flavour, gin derives its nose and taste from botanicals, which are simply natural herbs and spices such as coriander, orange and lemon peel, cinnamon, nutmeg, angelica and cardamom. Orris root is frequently used in more expensive products, not only for its flavour but because it acts to integrate and bind other flavours together. Botanical recipes, which may be of considerable age, are unique to each brand. These recipes are often a closely guarded secret, though some distillers, commendably in my view, print the details on their bottles or labels. Traditionally, no more than ten or a dozen botanicals would have been used; today, some recipes call for as many as forty-seven different herbs and spices. In recent years there has been a trend for distillers to experiment with ever more exotic or rare botanicals in an effort to develop new flavours and make their product stand out from the crowd. Increasingly, the requirement for juniper to predominate the taste has been ignored by producers of flavoured gins.

These range from essentially unremarkable (though pleasant) citrus-led gins such as Malfy con Limone to more *outré* expressions such as Shining Cliff's Bakewell Pud Gin (I am not making this up). Frankly, almost anything goes, and, while purists may be offended and suggest that many of these products are simply not gin but flavoured spirits, the wider market has embraced them. Even established brands such as Gordon's, Bombay Sapphire and Beefeater have belatedly joined the party, though most draw the line at relatively straightforward fruit additions. Only a few years ago this would have been unthinkable.

Distilled gin, once considered a lesser category but now more widely accepted, is made in a similar way to London gin, but the addition of further flavourings, both natural and artificial, is permitted on

How Gin is made at the Edinburgh Gin Distillery

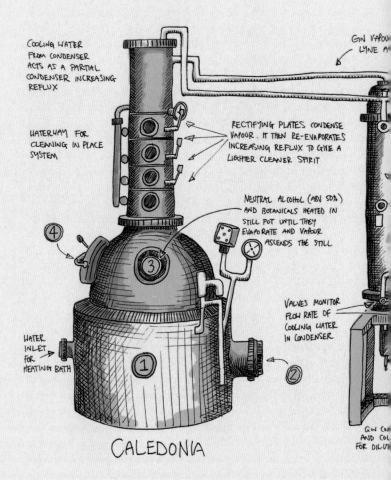

COOLING WATER FROM CONDENSER ACTS AS A PARTIAL CONDENSER INCREASING REFLUX

WATERWAY FOR CLEANING IN PLACE SYSTEM

RECTIFYING PLATES CONDENSE VAPOUR. IT THEN RE-EVAPORATES INCREASING REFLUX TO GIVE A LIGHTER CLEANER SPIRIT

NEUTRAL ALCOHOL (ABV 50%) AND BOTANICALS HEATED IN STILL POT UNTIL THEY EVAPORATE AND VAPOUR ASCENDS THE STILL

GIN VAPOUR LYNE A...

VALVES MONITOR FLOW RATE OF COOLING WATER IN CONDENSER

WATER INLET FOR HEATING BATH

GIN CO... AND COL... FOR DILU...

CALEDONIA

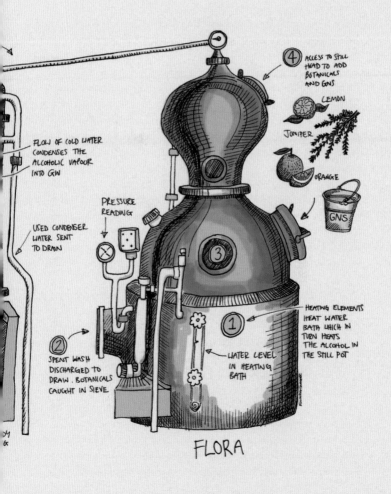

FLOW OF COLD WATER
CONDENSES THE
ALCOHOLIC VAPOUR
INTO GIN

USED CONDENSER
WATER SENT
TO DRAIN

PRESSURE
READING

④ ACCESS TO STILL
HEAD TO ADD
BOTANICALS
AND GNS

LEMON

JUNIPER

ORANGE

GNS

③

①

HEATING ELEMENTS
HEAT WATER
BATH WHICH IN
TURN HEATS
THE ALCOHOL IN
THE STILL POT

WATER LEVEL
IN HEATING
BATH

② SPENT WASH
DISCHARGED TO
DRAW . BOTANICALS
CAUGHT IN SIEVE

FLORA

completion of distillation. The legal minimum alcohol level in the EU is 37.5% alcohol by volume (abv), although most standard and premium brands are bottled and sold at a higher strength. This, of course, affects the price, not least because duty is charged according to the alcoholic content of the finished product. You will see the words 'Distilled Gin' on quite a few expressions from established brands – any stigma attached to the term seems to have vanished.

As gin, unlike whisky or brandy, does not require any maturation it may be bottled immediately, though many brands elect to 'rest' the spirit for some days or weeks to allow all the flavours to integrate fully. There has also been a recent trend to age gin in wooden casks to add colour and further develop flavour.

A third method is 'cold compounding', in which the essential oils from the botanicals are either distilled or simply pressed out and then added to the spirit. The resulting product may be labelled as 'gin', but not 'distilled' or 'London' gin. While in the past this method would have been reserved for cheaper, lower-quality products, there are today some more interesting and innovative expressions made in this way by smaller producers.

Brief mention should be made of the cold vacuum method, which often uses a piece of laboratory apparatus known as a rotary evaporator (or 'rota-vap'). By distilling under a vacuum, significantly lower temperatures may be used. It is argued that the more subtle and volatile elements of certain botanicals are thereby preserved and the resulting spirit is fresher and more vibrant in taste. A number of smaller producers are now making gin in this way.

Last but not least, it is worth noting that the biggest gin market in the world is the Philippines, accounting for more than 40% of global sales. The local favourite, by a country mile, is Ginebra San Miguel, but, because it is rarely seen beyond its home territory, I've elected to leave it out.

While writing this book I quickly lost count of the number of producers, particularly small ones, who had found a dusty old recipe from a hitherto long-forgotten gin-soaked ancestor that they felt compelled by some mysterious force to recreate, assured me of the 'passion' of their founders and wanted to tell me of their 'journey' and the 'hand-crafted' and 'artisanal' nature of their brand, evidently in the belief that this made them stand out in some way. It does not!

So, to help you through the confusion, I've suggested a selection of Essential Gins; turned briefly to tonic; taken a look at the most recent trend to 'pink' and flavoured gins; showcased some critical cocktails; and, doffing my hat to Scotland, where more than two-thirds of British gin is distilled (jings!) highlighted just a few of the new entrepreneurial producers to be found north of Hadrian's Wall.

What follows is the essential information: a large picture of the bottle; information on the distillery; the strength of the principal style; and where to find more information (naturally, the brands all have their own websites). There then follows my entirely personal description of what interested me about the particular product: it may be the people, the story, the history, the production method, the packaging or, sometimes, even the taste.

I have not offered scores. These are only ever one individual's opinion and I doubt that mine are consistent over time, but mainly I don't want my personal preferences and judgements to influence your decision to try any one of these products.

Finally, please remember the words of the American writer Roy Blount Jr: 'A good heavy book holds you down. It's an anchor that keeps you from getting up and having another gin and tonic.'

Botanicals ready for distilling at Sipsmith (juniper berries, bottom left).

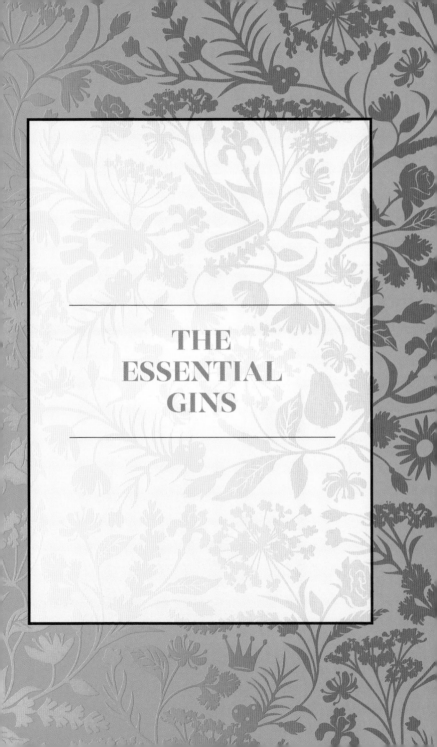

THE
ESSENTIAL
GINS

58 GIN

Distillery:	329 Acton Mews, London
Website:	www.58gin.com
Visitor Centre:	Yes
Strength:	43%

When I first encountered this in early 2015, it was probably the UK's newest gin brand and I knew at once that it had to go into a book. It's still around and going from strength to strength, so 58 stands as a great example of the new wave of small operations who have found a gap in the market. It typifies how gin is changing and why it's the most exciting thing on the world spirits scene right now.

Originally, it was the brainchild of a genial Aussie, Mark Marmont, an avid cocktail lover who, after a year of trials, lots of distilling courses and, as he says himself, 'trial and error', launched 58 – making just sixty to seventy bottles of gin at a time in a tiny copper pot still in a railway arch in Hackney Downs, one of the trendier parts of London. Since then, as I was informed by a robotically-voiced PR person in tones that did not invite further enquiry, Mark has 'exited the business and left the industry'.

However, we all move on, and 58 has now relocated to a new, larger home (albeit another railway arch) in Haggerston, also a seriously hip location. The current operation places great stress on their ethical operation and a mission 'to be the category leader in sustainable craft spirits'. To that end, they work closely with a Kent farm to source ingredients, they offset their carbon footprint by planting juniper bushes, and use the waste botanicals for compost, in a 'full green' circle they term 'ethical distilling'. Naturally, the packaging is eco-friendly, using recycled glass bottles and providing the on-trade with refill pouches to minimise waste.

This isn't unique, but it is the future and a great example of responsible industry that we should all encourage, support and emulate. The approach is also behind some great products, so much so that 58 collected no less than eight awards at the 2020 International Wine & Spirit Competition, including UK Gin Producer of the Year. That's a very respectable haul from a competition judged blind by industry experts.

Just as the distillery has expanded, so has the range. As well as their flagship London Dry, look out for 58's Apple and Hibiscus, English Berry and Navy Strength variants.

I just hope Mark's okay because he was fun to chat with and not unbearably woke.

ACHROOUS

Distillery:	The Tower Street Stillhouse, Leith, Edinburgh
Website:	www.electricspirit.co/gin
Visitor Centre:	No
Strength:	41%

In the Scotland of my long-lost youth there was a beverage known as 'Electric Soup'. Originally said to consist of milk with natural gas bubbled through it, it was the drink of down-and-outs and ne'er-do-wells – the sort of backdoor 'voddie' Rab C. Nesbitt might resort to on a particularly bad day.

So, Electric Spirit seems a curious name for a distillery in Leith, an area which has in recent years attained yuppie status by means of some muscular regeneration (i.e. the wholesale demolition of much of the old townscape to be replaced by bland 'designer' flats and a soulless shopping complex). Leith was once the haunt of thirsty sailors on shore leave and legions of accommodating ladies of the night. Today, it's all Michelin star-aspiring foodie restaurants, trendy bars and distraught Hibs fans clinging to fading memories of the 2016 Scottish Cup Final, with just a hint of the tantalising possibility of imminent random violence to remind one of the Leith of old. Even Hibs win things from time to time these days – but as their hardened fans bitterly observe, it's the hope that kills you.

But the Electric Spirit folks are no shrinking violets, otherwise why put their gin in a day-glo orange bottle (glance left if you don't believe me) and name it Achroous? That's not some strange Scottish war cry, by the way; it's derived from the Ancient Greek for 'colourless', which of course it is. To their eternal credit, they once produced a one-off release called Not Another Effing Gin. Believe me, writing about gin that's something I can acknowledge with feeling.

Electric Spirit are at the cutting edge of a vibrant Scottish craft-distilling scene, and product designer, photographer and distiller James Porteous has worked with juniper, coriander seed, orris root, liquorice root, angelica root, fennel seed and, most notably, Sichuan peppercorns to offer up this most distinctive spiced and complex gin, with attractive citrus and floral notes. Right from their 2015 launch, it sold well, allowing Electric Spirit to move to larger premises and acquire a bigger Genio still.

The Tower Street Stillhouse also produces the Port of Leith Distillery's excellent Lind & Lime gin, but to prove really good things come from here, I point you to Achroous' medal collection: Double Gold from the San Francisco World Spirits Awards, a 96pt Gold from the IWSC and Gold from the Spirits Business Global Gin Masters.

ADNAMS
COPPER HOUSE

Distillery:	Copper House Distillery, Southwold, Suffolk
Website:	www.adnams.co.uk
Visitor Centre:	Yes
Strength:	40%

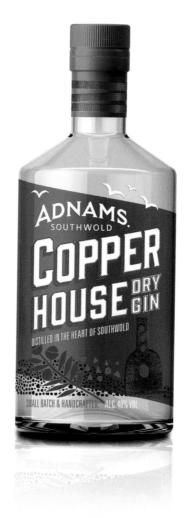

I suppose if you've been brewing great beer since 1872 and operate more than seventy pubs and an off-licence chain, then starting to distil your own range of spirits isn't the greatest leap in the dark. And with your own outlets to provide a ready market, it's probably a sound commercial move, yet it took Adnams until 2010 to start making vodka, gin, whisky and a range of liqueurs.

But, as you'd expect from their reputation as brewers, they've made a pretty decent job of it (I've tasted the whisky and it's excellent; I haven't the faintest idea about their vodka as I have a special dispensation never to touch the stuff).

Both vodka and gin start life as unhopped beer from the Adnams brewery. A column still is used to produce the high-strength vodka that then forms the spirit base for the gin. Botanicals (up to thirteen for the premium First Rate style) are added to the beefy 1,000-litre pot and redistilled with no further use of the columns (there is a very clear explanation of this on the website).

The equipment was all new and state of the art when installed in 2009, which is one advantage of starting from scratch, with decent capital behind you. The result is a clean, very elegant and classic London Dry gin that mixes well and has already collected a number of top awards (though as we shall see, not all awards are to be regarded equally highly).

It is, I would judge, more a classic G&T gin than a cocktail base, with six no-nonsense botanicals; though hibiscus might be considered a bit 'new wave' there is nothing else in there to upset your inner colonel. The higher-strength First Rate employs an additional eight botanicals but drops the hibiscus, thus making thirteen in all. However, to be honest, I preferred Copper House.

If you get the chance to visit Southwold, grab it and do not let go. After you've visited the brewery and distillery (there are various tours to take), the town itself is quite charming; the beach huts are fun to ogle (especially after you realise the prices at which they change hands); and the pier is worth the trip on its own. You can get great fish; you're only a few miles from Snape Maltings for some culture; and sitting on the beach at Southwold, gin and tonic in hand, watching the rolling waves and passing clouds is one of the great pleasures in life.

ASIAN PARSNIP

Distillery:	English Spirit, Great Yeldham, Essex
Website:	www.jamesgin.com
Visitor Centre:	No. But James May is part-owner of The Royal Oak, Swallowcliffe, Wilts.
Strength:	40%

L ate middle-aged celebrity launches own gin. Hardly news, is it? (Beats even older and lesser-known bloke writes book, though).

James May is probably best known as the co-presenter of *Top Gear* and more recently *The Grand Tour* but has also fronted programmes on science and technology and has published widely. He's also a decent musician, part-owner of a pub, and now he's created his own gin, 1,420 bottles of the launch edition selling out in under 24 hours. I'm starting to go off the bloke.

There's an excellent short video, in his distinctive faux self-deprecating style, on the FoodTribe YouTube channel, which explains why he did it but which also provides a simple and straightforward explanation of how gin is made, alongside distiller Hugh Anderson of the Downton Distillery, where Asian Parsnip was developed. Assuming it takes off as planned (and given May's following amongst middle-aged blokes, there's every reason to assume it will), future batches will be produced by the renowned Dr John Walters at the English Spirit distillery in Great Yeldham. Downton will provide a test-bed for new products, which is handy given that it's less than 20 miles from The Royal Oak, May's pub.

Like his motoring shows, May's Asian Parsnip is a joint enterprise with two colleagues – Gus Colquhoun and Will Daws (MD of a TV production house behind a number of May's programmes). But the idea for the project came from May himself, on the basis that his mum had given him a taste for gin, he owned half a pub and reckoned himself to be 'highly qualified in drinking gin, [having] done so all over the globe'. I suppose that'll do.

As the name suggests, this gin is a multi-cultural fusion of English and Asian influences with a botanicals mix including parsnips (that's the English bit which May describes, rather harshly I feel, as 'dowdy'), coriander, lemon and lime peels for their citrus impact, Sichuan pink peppercorns, angelica root and juniper. The use of parsnips may be unusual, but they're a tasty vegetable with hints of a woody forest floor and are an inspired addition to the botanical repertoire. Not dowdy at all.

And now, the best bit. As they say on the website, here are some of the words they DON'T use: Deconstructed, Artisanal, Craft, Curated and Authentic. And, Dionysus be praised, the dreaded p-word (see p. 189) doesn't appear either. For that alone, you have to try this.

AUDEMUS PINK PEPPER

Distillery:	4 Rue du Pont Faumet, 16100 Cognac, France
Website:	www.audemus-spirits.com
Visitor Centre:	Visits possible by special arrangement
Strength:	44%

Any company based in the very heart of Cognac, founded by an Australian and managed by two fellows styling themselves Director of Capers and Director of Doing, must be worthy of consideration, even though the distillery is less than ten years old. Despite that, it has made quite an impact on the French craft-distilling scene, attracting the attention of the more innovative cocktail mixologists and collecting major awards in international competition.

What we find is quite an unusual set-up: separate reduced pressure; low temperature distillation of each ingredient (rather like Sacred); and the use of some unconventional botanicals that include honey (rather like Dodd's), vanilla, tonka beans and the pink peppercorns that give the gin its name.

Distiller Miko Abouaf (he's the Australian by the way and the Director of Capers – not the salty little berries often found in cooking but suggestive of frivolity and jolly larking about) had spent some time working in Cognac but wanted to create his own aromatic gin built upon a juniper base. His goal was to create a product with a complexity that will develop and evolve over time, both in bottle and in the glass. The juniper base gives the gin a classical integrity but other notes emerge. The tonka beans enhance the effect of the vanilla (I'll admit here that I had to look those beans up as I'd never heard of the things) and, served at room temperature or gently warmed, the overall impact is delightfully reminiscent of a fragrant pâtisserie: certainly a gin that you can sip with pleasure.

But served over ice or in a suitable cocktail, spicy notes from juniper and cardamom are more obviously apparent. This is where the pink peppercorn comes in, but first understand that the name is something of a misnomer: this is actually a dried berry fruit. However, it does look rather like a peppercorn once dried and has something of a peppery taste, hence its title.

Audemus is not the only distiller using this botanical – both Durham Gin and Tarquin's in the UK are fans – but it is somewhat unorthodox. As it grows wild in Australia, perhaps it was a taste of home for Miko, but whatever the reason for its inclusion, it certainly works well here, balancing the warmth and smooth mouthfeel of the locally sourced honey. A very impressive product, and attractively presented.

AVIATION

Distillery:	Portland, Oregon
Website:	www.aviationgin.com
Visitor Centre:	Under development
Strength:	42%

H ere's a new American gin that really polarises opinion. For the most part, people – especially mixologists – rave about it. It's picked up prestigious accolades from top magazines and enjoys a generally stellar reputation. What's more, global drinks giant Diageo liked it so much that in August 2020 they lashed out a cool $335m to buy it, with another $275m to follow if sales lived up to expectations.

Mind you, that may be as much about Diageo's star-struck management as any special merits of the liquid. Aviation was part-owned by actor Ryan Reynolds, and Diageo have form in celebrity tie-ins – think David Beckham with Haig Club and George Clooney's Casamigos tequila, both following in the footsteps of Sean Coombs (aka Puff Daddy or P. Diddy) and Ciroc vodka. It's clearly a marketing route that works.

But some folk don't like the liquid. One comment I saw on noted blog site theginisin.com read: 'I poured mine down the drain. I made a martini with it and it was so vile, I didn't even eat the olives.' That's pretty damning and certainly not worth millions of dollars.

Though I do think it lacks subtlety, that does seem harsh. It seems somewhat unbalanced with a coarse and unappealing nose and a crude herbal note to the taste. Of the orange and floral hints detected by other tasters I could find no hint. But – and I can't say this often enough – this is just one person's opinion and it's why you won't find any scores here. Many other judges would disagree quite forcefully and I wouldn't want to put you off trying it.

To be fair, Aviation was an early pioneer in the craft gin movement and deserves a lot of credit for that. It's the creation of a very well-known Seattle mixologist Ryan Magarian in collaboration with the House Spirits Distillery in Portland, Oregon. After a series of trials, they came up with the Aviation recipe, named it after a classic gin cocktail, and launched the product in June 2006, since when it has enjoyed international success.

It was part of a very deliberate move away from classic, juniper-led English gins which have become known as 'American Gin' or 'New Western Dry Gin', and, if you like a forceful, straight-to-the-point gin, this may be for you.

But whatever you and I may think, Mr Reynolds clearly doesn't have to worry about his grocery bills any longer!

BARRA
ATLANTIC

Distillery:	Castlebay, Isle of Barra
Website:	www.isleofbarradistillers.com
Visitor Centre:	Café and shop
Strength:	46%

This town ain't big enough for the both of us ... or should that be island? Who'd imagine that on an isolated Outer Hebridean island – so remote that aeroplanes land on the beach (when the tide is out, obvs) – there could be a face-off between the Isle of Barra Distillers and their long-established rivals Uisge Beatha nan Eilean. My local spy speaks of native botanicals such as rue, acrimony and bitter gall springing up everywhere.

Since 2005 there have been ambitions for a distillery but, despite the recent generally favourable investment climate, the original plan's promoters have been unable to arrange finance and their scheme appears to have stalled. Enter Katie and Michael Morrison, who arrived in 2016 and got their operation in Castlebay planned, built, opened and making gin by May 2019. Of course, whisky is the big dream, as Barra is famed as the original *Whisky Galore* island, but gin is a very good place to start.

So, congratulations to the Isle of Barra Distillers with their tasty and beautifully packaged Barra Atlantic Gin. It has a stylish marbling effect on the label which drew me in immediately. What's more, they've installed an impressive copper still from Forsyths (noted for their whisky stills but making great gin as well – see Bluecoat in Philadelphia) and have cleverly worked locally sourced carrageen, a type of edible seaweed, into their seventeen botanicals.

The result is a single-minded gin with plenty of juniper notes that will appeal to traditionalists and drinkers looking for something just a little bit different. I respect the single-minded focus on just one variety and the energy and drive that has brought them this far. They've recently been chosen as the house pour at Glasgow's renowned Two Fat Ladies at the Buttery restaurant which, given the gins already distilled on the restaurant's doorstep, is no mean feat.

A further claim to fame is that they are Scotland's most westerly distillery, though it must be a close-run contest with North Uist. Actually, I'm never very sure why these claims, which come up again and again, matter in the slightest, but as it seems important to them, I thought I'd pass it on.

Rather more significantly, they've recruited Alan Winchester, a former Master Distiller at The Glenlivet (and all-round nice guy), to advise on the development of their whisky. So, look out, because they're clearly determined and shrewd people who deserve to succeed.

BECKETTS

Distillery:	Kingston Distillers Ltd, 28 Portsmouth Road, Kingston upon Thames, London
Website:	www.beckettsgin.co.uk
Visitor Centre:	No
Strength:	40%

One of the loveliest things about loving gin at the moment is that you can enjoy your favourite tipple *and* a glow of virtue. Gins – well, some gins – have a social conscience. One shares its profits to help gorillas and another to protect elephants.

In this case, charity begins at home: Beckett's, which uses hand-picked juniper berries from Box Hill in Surrey (the setting, you will recall, for a famous, if unhappy, picnic in Jane Austen's *Emma*), is working with the National Trust, Forest Research and Natural England to help save juniper from extinction in England. A worthy cause, you may feel, and one close to the heart of all true gin lovers. If it works, juniper will once again flourish on Juniper Top, Surrey.

For a relatively new company, launching its signature gin as recently as 2014, this is a bold and noteworthy initiative, giving it bragging rights as the only gin made using English juniper. For the moment, that is, as Vicars Gin from Worcestershire have recently started growing their own. However, as the bushes take several years to mature, Beckett's unique claim seems safe for a little while. It is, however, a necessarily small-scale operation, hence there is no visitor centre or access to the distillery. As founder Neil Beckett explains, this is 'a home-based business so there are no plans to have visitors until we relocate'.

The other distinctive note here comes from the use of Kingston upon Thames mint as a botanical – sweet yet cooling, it harmonises with just four other ingredients in a deceptively simple formula that results in a mix of zesty citrus (lime and sweet orange peel) and earthy spice (orris and coriander). Mint is the recommended garnish, as perhaps it should be; it's grown at the distillery's home.

There's a puzzling reference on the label to 'Type 1097'. Surely they didn't have 1,096 prior attempts at the recipe? I knew you'd want to know, so I enquired and the answer is that it is their first gin (hence 1) and this was the ninety-seventh attempt to perfect the recipe. I don't suppose 'Type 197' has quite the same ring to it!

There are three styles: Type 1097, Sloe Gin and the bold 48% Spirited London Dry. Local juniper, local mint, local artwork on the label, your cash helps save English juniper and the brand even sponsors a gin quiz at their local gastropub. Splendid stuff.

BEEFEATER DRY

Distillery:	Beefeater, Kennington, London
Website:	www.beefeatergin.com
Visitor Centre:	Yes
Strength:	40%

Since 2005, when the French drinks giant Pernod Ricard acquired the Beefeater brand and distillery, things have been looking up for this great old brand – for years the last branded flag-carrier for London-distilled London Dry. They've poured both money and love (the latter every bit as important as the cash) into developing both distillery and brand. Their urbane and unflappable Master Distiller Desmond Payne MBE, arguably the world's most experienced gin distiller, is clearly loving every moment of this well-deserved high point in his distinguished career.

But gin lovers have long recognised the quality behind its iconic label (though, as an aside, I do wish those restless young creatives would stop messing about with their torrent of 'limited edition' label designs – if it ain't broke, don't fix it). In many ways, this would be the gin I'd recommend to someone who only had room for one gin in their cupboard and was watching the pennies. Frankly, it's great value, and all things considered it's hard to beat for an authentic gin taste. I continue to refer to it as my reference point as a gold standard for gin.

Recently, the distillery benefited from the development of a small but rather handsome visitor centre (£16, but that includes a G&T) which traces the history of gin, with particular emphasis on London's role, naturally. If you're sufficiently interested you can investigate the individual exhibits with the assistance of an iPad, or you can just stroll quickly through to the tasting that awaits. Actually, that would be a shame, because the displays, going right back to the brand's first home, the Chelsea Distillery of 1820, subsequently purchased by Beefeater's founder, James Burrough, are fun and very well done.

In the inevitable shop you can pick up a bottle of Beefeater's harder-to-find expressions including the premium 24 (45% with extra tea and citrus botanicals) and Burrough's Reserve, a 'barrel rested' aged gin distilled in a tiny nineteenth-century copper still, or browse the growing selection of speciality gins, including London Garden, Monday's Gin, Crown Jewel, Beefeater Pink Strawberry, Blood Orange, Blackberry or Peach & Raspberry. Let no one say that established brands can't innovate and explore the flavour possibilities of a quality gin.

In fact, ubiquitous and inexpensive it may be, but Beefeater is a classic. Until you've tried it, you're not really a gin drinker.

BERRY BROS. & RUDD LONDON DRY

Distillery:	Thames Distillers, Timbermill Distillery, Clapham, London
Website:	www.bbr.com
Visitor Centre:	No, but a lovely shop at 3 St James's Street, Mayfair, London
Strength:	40.6%

A blast from the past? After all, what more traditional, upper-crust symbol of London could one find than Berry Bros. & Rudd's delightfully antiquated shop at Mayfair's 3 St James's Street? Over three centuries of tradition seep from its storied walls. They have long supplied the British ruling classes' thirst with claret and other fine beverages, and were responsible for creating Cutty Sark, one of the great cocktail whiskies.

So, naturally, they have a gin. Actually, they have several, starting with the traditional, juniper-led No. 3 London Dry. But there's a slight problem. Its bottle gives the hint, for it's in the shape of an old-fashioned genever. Which hails from the Low Countries, not London. And it turns out that this very fine, inimitably English gin is, in fact, distilled for Berry's in Holland, which, of course, is where gin's story started (unless, perchance, you buy Malfy's version).

However, now – drum roll, please – they offer a London Dry actually made in London. And it's my 'blast from the past', because this is a recreation of Berry's Best, the gin they were selling as long ago as 1909 and a product highly praised by David Embury (a giant amongst cocktail writers) as representing 'superior British gin production'. But it was a casualty of gin's sorry decline after the Second World War and only one bottle survived in BB&R's hallowed cellars.

Could it be cloned? They turned to Master Distiller Charles Maxwell, modest gin superstar and the man behind many of the smaller brands we all adore. With one tiny sample to work with, Maxwell's venerable John Dore stills – Tom Thumb and Thumbelina (London-made, naturally) – were soon in action and the legend was reborn.

This is a taste of history, a junipery London Dry classic. Forget exotic fruit infusions; eschew lengthy lists of obscure botanicals; shun the capricious and wilfully neoteric; this is the gin that our forefathers drank (always assuming they could afford to shop at BB&R). Great decisions that affected the fate of nations were likely made over large London Dry G&Ts in the more exclusive recesses of London's clubland, though I cannot help observing several flavoured variants which once might have resulted in an H. M. Bateman moment in those hallowed halls.

No longer. In our more democratic age, this is a little bit of a bargain: a good fiver and change cheaper than their No. 3 and made in London to boot. Chin, chin!

BLUECOAT

Distillery:	Philadelphia Distilling, Philadelphia, Pennsylvania, USA
Website:	www.bluecoatgin.com
Visitor Centre:	Yes
Strength:	47%

Bluecoat is a perfect example of the new contenders that are revitalising gin's image – and taste. Using their own custom-designed still, specially crafted by Forsyths in Scotland, Philadelphia Distilling have aimed from the get-go to make what they call American Dry Gin, in a style that is all their own. For a small start-up, the company have enjoyed some considerable success and, though they concentrate on the US market, supplies have made it to the UK.

Their neutral grain spirit is redistilled five times in their pot still, and the use of organic American juniper provides an earthy base to the nose and flavour, while the distinctive signature of Bluecoat is a citrus note derived (I believe) from grapefruit peel, though the distiller would neither confirm nor deny my theory.

Though now established for more than fifteen years and part of the Samson & Surrey boutique spirits operation, the company is still largely run by the energetic and committed original team, who were pioneering and enthusiastic enough to establish Pennsylvania's first legal distillery since Prohibition. Based first in an industrial unit on the edge of the city, they have since moved all their distilling and bottling operations to a new, larger site located in the hipster neighbourhood of Fishtown – 'the hottest neighbourhood in the USA' according to a recent issue of *Forbes* magazine – and opened a visitor centre. Enlightened new legislation makes it possible to retail their products direct to the public and offer distillery tours – vital promotional activity for a company of this scale.

Having had the opportunity to visit both sites, I'm impressed by what has been done in their distinctly cool new home and the impact it's having on the regeneration of a once gritty part of town.

The Bluecoat name emphasises the robustly American nature of this gin, being based on the nickname of the militia of the American War of Independence (or Revolutionary War, as the beastly colonists insist on calling it), hence the company's slogan 'Be Revolutionary'. It's very far from revolting, though, and even a true Brit can enjoy Bluecoat's cleansing, refreshing taste and 47% abv strength. The Barrel Reserve is a small-batch release, aged in American oak barrels for a full twelve months, which are used only twice. I find the slightly fuller flavour works agreeably well in a Negroni, and look out, too, for the zesty Elderflower expression as Bluecoat continue their welcome expansion into international markets.

BOMBAY SAPPHIRE

Distillery:	Bombay Spirits Company, Laverstoke, Hampshire
Website:	www.bombaysapphire.com
Visitor Centre:	Yes
Strength:	40%

Like a number of other currently fashionable gins, Bombay Sapphire relies on its retro-style packaging to persuade us it's been around for ages. In one sense it has, in that the base recipe (as used in the Original Dry variant) dates back to 1761 when it was known as Warrington Dry Gin. It did not appear in its Bombay guise until 1960, and Sapphire, which added two botanicals to the recipe, was launched only in 1987.

It has a decent claim to saving the entire gin category, here and in the USA. A new wave of innovative bartenders, led by the legendary Dick Bradsell (inventor of the Bramble cocktail and mentor to today's tattooed 'mixologists'), picked up on Sapphire's light, fresh and delicate nose and taste, and began to look at gin in an exciting new way.

It took a little while for this to gather momentum, but a number of competitors followed, chief amongst them Hendrick's. Today, it seems that new gins, ultimately inspired by Sapphire, appear almost weekly.

In 1997, the brand was acquired by Bacardi. Until 2014, production remained at Warrington, where it was distilled under contract by G. & J. Greenall, but today it has its own home at the splendid Laverstoke Mill, where a magnificent visitor centre has been built. I'll simply urge you to go without delay.

There you can stroll through the very attractive grounds, gasp at the soaring glasshouses designed by Thomas Heatherwick, learn all about botanicals, and design your own cocktail, but, best of all, you can see the highly unusual Carterhead stills which aim to preserve the fresh character of the botanicals through the vapour infusion method of distilling. The result is a subtle and delicate spirit, which, though light in character, does not lack complexity or charm. Production has been greatly expanded by the multi-million-pound move to Laverstoke, but great care has been taken to ensure absolute continuity of flavour under the direction of Master Distiller Dr Anne Brock and colleague Ivano Tonutti, Master of Botanicals.

Today, there are a number of variants. You might care for the fruity Bramble, but for a knock-your-socks-off gin, what you really want is the export strength Sapphire (47%) as found at the airport, which is a superbly rewarding component of a good cocktail, or the exotic Star of Bombay with its beguiling pepper and lemongrass notes. Then you can raise a glass to the gin which, almost single-handedly, rescued gin!

BOND STREET

Distillery:	Bond Street Distillery, Hinckley, Leicestershire
Website:	www.thebondstreetdistillery.co.uk
Visitor Centre:	Yes
Strength:	40%

Like a number of its counterparts, the Bond Street Distillery finds its home in repurposed industrial buildings, survivors of Victorian enterprise. It's great to see these old factories, once a hive of industry and a source of employment, brought back to life rather than being demolished for bland and characterless housing or yet another retail shed. It restores life to often run-down areas and, along with other small craft and artisan-based businesses, can be the key to a vibrant regeneration that builds a youthful new community where once weeds and litter filled the streets.

I have some knowledge of the trials and tribulations involved in building projects, especially the restoration of old structures, so I truly have the greatest of respect for anyone taking on such a task while simultaneously attempting to build a new business from the ground up. So kudos to Sally Faulkner and her team for everything that's been done at the Bond Street Distillery.

Since going on site in September 2018 the progress has been impressive, and now, from some proper German stills, a fine range of gins is starting to flow. The choice of stills reveals a professional approach that's further emphasised when we learn that Jamie Baxter, formerly of Chase and Burleighs and now a flying ginmaker consultant (he calls it 'work'), helped set up the stills and also trained Bond Street's Head Distiller Ed Gibson. These are all good signs.

So what do they offer? In short, an impressive, well-packaged and imaginatively created range of small-batch gins. Leading off is their signature London Dry, with the ranks completed with a Navy Strength expression and three flavoured gins. Blood Orange and Raspberry are seen often enough, but I think Rhubarb and Custard may be a first.

It makes sense though, and like everything here has clearly been properly thought out. Rhubarb is quintessentially English (other gins do feature it) and lends a sharp sweetness to gin. But here it's tempered by the creamy vanilla of real custard, making for a genuinely innovative twist on what is rapidly becoming a classic amongst new wave gins.

Their Bond Street Social is a bar, tasting room, music venue and event space at the heart of the distillery. Others might look enviously at this converted hosiery factory and realise they have to pull their socks up!

BOTANIST

Distillery:	Bruichladdich, Islay
Website:	www.thebotanist.com
Visitor Centre:	Yes
Strength:	46%

This is what happens when a small, rather isolated whisky distillery that is not without a sense of its own importance makes gin. It's lovely and, as things turned out, destined for global success.

The Botanist is made on Islay by Bruichladdich – self-styled 'progressive Hebridean distillers'. They do bang on a bit about how they're different from everyone else, though in many ways they are. Their near-obsessive fans awarded them cult status. In recent years, following a July 2012 acquisition by Rémy Cointreau, they've shed the *enfant terrible* pose, which was getting a trifle wearing (at least I thought so) and have matured somewhat. In their new, grown-up way, the distillery is now certified as a B-Corp and manages The Botanist Foundation, a Community Interest Company which funds biodiversity and conservation work across five continents.

But they always did fun, unexpected and offbeat things. Such an attitude lay behind their last-minute recovery of one of the very few surviving true Lomond stills left anywhere in the world shortly before it was scrapped. Originally designed in the late 1950s as a sort of compromise between a pot and column, the Lomond still was intended for Scotch whisky. Sadly though, it never really worked satisfactorily and, like the dustbin it resembles, was destined for the waste basket of whisky history.

However, Bruichladdich's then Master Distiller Jim McEwan realised that, if run very slowly, it could be ideal for making gin and so he adapted the still to include a separate container for the botanicals (sourced, of course, uniquely on Islay), thus working the Lomond apparatus as a sort of hybrid Carterhead. Head Distiller Adam Hannett is now in charge.

It's not, let it be said, a particularly good-looking piece of kit. In fact, the distillery affectionately named it 'Ugly Betty' and once painted a rather voluptuous Virgin Atlantic-style lady onto the column (she's gone now, presumably to avoid triggering the more sensitive visitors).

As for the gin itself, a fairly standard range of botanicals is infused with the base spirit and then augmented by passing the vapour through a further twenty-two more delicate island botanicals. The result is a complex, robust yet floral gin of great charm. Rémy Cointreau bought Bruichladdich for their single malt whisky, but ten years on from its birth, The Botanist is sold in sixty-six countries and is one of the best-selling super premium gins in the world. Turns out it was the real bargain.

BOXER

Distillery:	The Langley Distillery, Langley Green, Warley, West Midlands
Website:	www.boxergin.com
Visitor Centre:	No
Strength:	40%

You think this is called Boxer because it was reputedly inspired by gin-loving Victorian pugilist Tom King or because there's a picture of a boxer on the bottle, don't you? Well, it might be … but I have another theory. It may just be that it's because it comes in a box. Clever, eh?

Not for you and me, you understand; we just get it in a bottle, like any old other gin, and, as you'd expect, there is indeed an illustration of two strapping fellows engaged in fisticuffs right there on the front. But if you run a bar and order Boxer, after you've got some empty bottles your second and subsequent orders can come in a nifty 2.8 litre Eco-Pouch in a box.

According to parent company The Sustainable Spirit Co., it's the most environmentally friendly way to buy spirits, given that the Eco-Pouch contains the equivalent of four bottles of gin but costs 20% less. Refilling a bottle from an Eco-Pouch also produces over a kilogram less CO_2 than buying a new bottle.

All you have to do as the bar owner is keep your empties, carefully refill them, and sit back, luxuriating sanctimoniously in a sense of your green virtue. I'm not aware of any other company doing this but a zero-waste refill and reuse system must be the future. As well as a bit of a bargain if you were just having a party.

However, it may be green, but is it any good? Well, if you like a pronounced juniper hit on your gin, then yes it is. Boxer separately distil fresh wild juniper berries at source in the Himalayas and cold-press their bergamot peel, adding these extracts to a classic London Dry gin distilled by Langley's of Birmingham (their renowned 'Angela' still is in action here). This means it may only be described as a 'distilled gin' but it ensures a very fresh, forceful and vibrant delivery of the key flavours, which are long-lasting and stand up well to dilution with tonic or in a cocktail.

Sipped neat, the flavours in Boxer are perhaps too assertive for some, so this is something of a heavyweight amongst gins – to borrow a memorable phrase, it floats like a butterfly but stings like a bee.

Meanwhile, don't forget about Langley's who we shall meet again. They're an important part of gin's revival.

BRIGHTON

Distillery:	The Gin Cave, Portslade, Sussex
Website:	www.brightongin.com
Visitor Centre:	You can arrange a distillery visit but they are curiously coy and don't release the address until you have booked!
Strength:	40%

The late, great Keith Waterhouse, novelist, author and a long-time resident of Brighton, once memorably declared that it had 'the air of a town helping the police with its inquiries'. It certainly carries a certain raffish manner, an *insouciant* attitude and a *fin-de-siècle* glamour that for years marked it out as the place to go for a dirty weekend, or perhaps for ill-matched couples in need of sham proof of adultery. To be fair, the Brighton Gin folk don't shy away from the image; in fact, the small print on the label rejoices in it.

Again and again, this image occurs in books: from *Pride and Prejudice* by way of *Vanity Fair*, *Brighton Rock* and *Sugar Rush* Brighton acts as a counterpoint to civilised (hah!) London, a veritable den of iniquity, sexual excess and casual violence. Not, I hasten to add, that anything at all exciting has ever happened to me on my all too fleeting visits ('and a jolly good thing, too' adds Mrs Buxton).

Gin seems Brighton's natural partner. What else would you drink on some illicit liaison than Mother's Ruin? So it's perhaps surprising that no one had thought to launch a Brighton Gin. Even if it were distilled somewhere else, Brighton's glitzy allure would surely have exercised a fascination for even the most *outré* of drinkers and injected a *soupçon* of hitherto unsuspected debauchery into the image of the most drably respectable of provincial chartered accountants.

So, it had to be done, and Kathy Caton and chums made the first move. Loving Brighton as they do, the cheery labelling, with its hints of the fairground, was inspired by the city itself and the distinctive Brighton seafront blue that appears on railings and bus shelters. Was that risky or simply *risqué*?

Since its launch, Brighton has gone on from strength to strength. On which note, in addition to the regular 40% 'Pavilion Strength' they also produce a somewhat heftier 'Seaside Naval Strength' at 57%. If such things concern you, it may be of interest that this is the UK's first contemporary Vegan Society-accredited gin, meaning that not just the liquid inside but every aspect of the bottle from the wax seal on top to the glue on the labels is certified 100% vegan.

Finally, then, something you can bring home from London-by-the-Sea that you can safely share with your mother-in-law.

BROKER'S

Distillery:	The Langley Distillery, Langley Green, Warley, West Midlands
Website:	www.brokersgin.com
Visitor Centre:	No
Strength:	40%

Does anyone still wear a bowler hat? Isn't the little plastic hat on top of this bottle, and even the name, simply a bit of a gimmick? Well, yes, but then the company themselves shamelessly admit that this is a brand with 'a decidedly playful spirit'.

And what's wrong with a bit of fun, you might ask. At little more than twenty quid, this would make a splendid present (I wouldn't turn it down). If you splash out just a little more, you can afford their 47% export strength but check the label carefully if that's not what you want; they are very similarly packaged and easily confused (until you start drinking, that is).

But is the gin any good? I hear you cry. Well, if awards are anything to go by, then, yes, it is. The website asserts that Broker's has won more top awards in international competitions over the last ten years than any other gin. Others might dispute that, and, as we shall see, there have been awards aplenty for different gins over the past few years.

The problem here for the unwitting consumer is award inflation. Brands have entered into a sort of arms race and, spotting an opportunity, lots of new awards have sprung up, happy to collect the entry fees and dish out gongs. Not all awards are of equal merit – you wouldn't consider a win in the one hundred metres at a school parents' day a match for Olympic gold – and the same applies to drinks awards so you have to treat them with some caution.

Not, I rush to say, that Broker's is anything other than a completely splendid and very fine libation, especially if you like a straightforward, traditional classic gin, which this is, most definitely and unapologetically. Distilled by Langley's in Angela, a good old John Dore pot still of a century and more's vintage, just ten botanicals are used. No surprises and nothing 'weird and wonderful' in the list; after all, as they say themselves, 'We believe our forefathers did an unbeatable job perfecting gin recipes over many hundreds of years.' No fancy fruit flavours here, not even an Old Tom (which the forefathers were rather partial to).

But single-minded is fair enough. If you're looking for a slightly offbeat gift for a gin connoisseur that won't break the bank, look no further. Broker's is it: you can take your hat off to it.

BROOKLYN

Distillery:	Warwick Valley Winery & Distillery, Warwick, New York State
Website:	www.brooklyngin.com
Visitor Centre:	No
Strength:	40%

Surely Brooklyn, New York, is the epitome of cool. Founded in 2010, the intention has always been to distil in the city, but, for the present, financial pressures mean that Brooklyn's production and bottling takes place at the Warwick Valley Distillery in Hudson Valley. And don't ever confuse it with Breuckelen gin which is distilled in Brooklyn – this being the land of the free, lawyers were soon involved in a spat over naming rights. Potato, potahto …

But since Brooklyn is hardly the only brand working with a third-party distillery, I think we can let them off with this minor geographic infelicity. This is a great example of American gin – with loads of citrus (think Bluecoat) as they pack the Carl still with fresh and hand-peeled key limes, lemon, lime and orange. And while on the hand-crafted note, it would be remiss not to note that the Albanian juniper berries are cracked by hand as well – these guys must have a firm handshake – so, if initially a little subdued, the pine note is there. Take a second sip and enjoy the subtle segue from citrus-led to juniper influence. This is clever stuff.

Refreshingly, given the trend for the early pioneers to sell up, Brooklyn remains independent in ownership. Despite the inevitable constraints this involves, they have achieved decent international distribution. Part of that success must be attributed to the very striking packaging: the heavy, green-tinted art deco-style bottle with its prominent bronze medallion really stands out on shelf and is satisfying to hold and pour (but it's heavy, so watch out). It's understated but authoritative. The copper cap has a neat trick: it's an ice stamp – simply press it on your ice cube and the logo appears. Result: very cool ice.

Hailing from the USA, this just has to work in cocktails and, no surprise, Brooklyn really hits its stride here. The website offers a helpful range and you shouldn't hesitate to experiment. It packs more of a punch than the 40% strength would suggest, with the pronounced citrus note holding up well after mixing.

Brooklyn has a hatful of worthwhile awards to its name, including Double Golds at both the San Francisco World Spirits Competition and the New York World Wine & Spirits Competition to put alongside various craft-distilling accolades. It's decent value for the presentation, and with all that citrus fruit it's definitely one to look out for.

BURLEIGH'S

Distillery:	Bawdon Lodge Farm, Leicestershire
Website:	www.burleighsgin.com
Visitor Centre:	Yes
Strength:	40%

I've just noticed that a lot of gins begin with the letter 'B'. Before you ask, I haven't the faintest idea why this is, but look how long it's taken us just to get here. What's more, Burleighs' original style (still in production) was created by a chap named Baxter. I think it's fate.

He appears to be moving backwards from the letter 'C'. That's not a cryptic clue, merely a reference to the fact that as Burleighs' Head Distiller Jamie Baxter began work at Chase Distillery, then moved on to City of London and has since established a consultancy to help other smaller distillers get started. However, day-to-day distilling is now carried out under the watchful eye of Charlie Hendon, another of the many women increasingly leading the distilling industry into the twenty-first century while Baxter continues as a flying distiller.

The name comes from the distillery's location near to Charnwood Forest and Burleigh Woods nature reserve. As the story goes, Jamie was walking there one day and was inspired by the local botanicals that he found – including silver birch, dandelion, burdock, elderberry and a few secret ingredients as well as some more conventional ones.

As to the signature expression, it's a fairly classic London Dry, well made and elegant. The nose is crisp, clean and fresh, with juniper and citrus coming through nice and early, an initial hit of juniper and pine with floral and spicy dry notes on tasting, followed by tart orange notes.

It's at the heart of an admirably tight core range of just three gins: the Leicester Dry is joined by the stronger Distiller's Cut and the Tokyo-inspired Pink Edition, where Japanese cherry blossom, hibiscus, rose and pink grapefruit are added to the base recipe.

Perhaps more intriguingly, Burleighs is the 'official gin partner' of Leicester City FC, Leicester Tigers RFC and the King Richard III Foundation, and they worked with the late Marilyn Monroe's estate to create a limited run of pink gin (in a pink bottle naturally). King Richard III of England died some centuries prior to his fellow gin icon, though is popularly remembered for the discovery of his remains in a Leicester car park. Older readers may remember Ms Monroe as an actress or for her sultry performance of 'Happy Birthday' for President John F. Kennedy. Worth four minutes of your time on You Tube and an hour or so contemplating the Twitter reaction had this happened today!

CANAÏMA

Distillery:	Destilerías Unidas S.A., Lara, Venezuela
Website:	www.canaimagin.com
Visitor Centre:	No
Strength:	47%

As you will see, many of the new gins on the block place great emphasis on their sustainability. Some are aiming for B-Corp certification, and many support charities working on environmental or animal conservation causes. Whether it's a mere genuflection in the direction of an increasingly woke marketplace or a mark of a deeper commitment, I couldn't say. In reality, it probably varies, but the general direction of travel for the spirits industry is something we can and should all applaud and support, both for the sake of the planet and for the generations that come after us. In that context, there is probably no bigger or more important cause than the protection of the Amazon rainforest. Enter Canaïma Gin, distilled in Venezuela by the people behind Diplomático rum and created in partnership with Simone Caporale, a top London cocktail specialist, who you may have seen on Jamie Oliver's Drinks Tube. Frankly, with such credentials, who needs more? But, as I have to fill this page, I'll continue.

It could just be more corporate greenwashing, but I really don't think so. After all, it's a cause very close to the distillery's home and employees. Named after Canaïma National Park, 10% of the profit from each bottle helps fund reforestation of the Amazon as well as preserving the culture and heritage of the indigenous people. In 2021 alone, they will replant at least 2,500 trees and support local businesses – a modest enough number given the scale of the problem but a positive start.

One of the famous 'known unknowns' is the contribution that the rainforest and the knowledge of the people living there could possibly make to modern medicine. Turns out that the fruits growing there can also do quite a lot for gin: out of some 3,000 varieties found locally Canaïma have selected ten as vital botanicals. They include açaí berries, uve de palma, copoazú, túpiro, merey, seje and semeruco – and, no, I've no idea either, but you can learn more on the brand's website. For now, just take it from me they taste great and make a very fine gin with plenty of depth, complexity and body.

There's much more on the website about the brand's mission with NGOs such as Saving the Amazon and the Fundación Tierra Viva alongside a handy guide to some cocktails from the man himself, which is worth checking out, as they don't all require frustratingly obscure or expensive ingredients.

CAORUNN

Distillery:	Balmenach, Cromdale, Moray
Website:	www.caorunngin.com
Visitor Centre:	No
Strength:	41.8%

An apple a day keeps the doctor away! Well, that's my excuse. Caorunn (say it 'ka-roon') recommend a slice of red apple in place of the more normal lime or lemon and I think that's probably a first. Is it just a gimmick, though?

Well, if lime or lemon are there to enhance gin's citrus flavours, the fact that Caorunn include the ancient Coul Blush variety of apples in their botanical line-up, alongside six classics such as juniper and coriander, could provide the justification. Mind you, they've got rowanberries in there as well (the trees keep witches away, at least according to Celtic folk tradition – and ever since I planted one I've never had a problem with over-friendly old hags at my front door), and bog myrtle and heather, not to mention dandelion. Quite apart from the fact that dandelion is a pernicious weed, albeit with a pretty flower, I believe we'll draw a veil over its alleged diuretic properties. I'm not at all certain what I'm expected to taste when encountering dandelion, though as we have already noted, it's also used in Burleighs gin.

By virtue of its parent Inver House Distillers, who have a range of single malt whiskies, Caorunn have achieved wider distribution than many other small gin brands. They've also collected a number of decent awards. What's more interesting is that it's made at Balmenach, a small single malt whisky distillery on Speyside that dates back to 1824, but using a dedicated gin still. Around 1,000 litres of triple-distilled grain spirit are used in each batch, the spirit vapour being passed through a unique copper Berry Chamber that dates to the 1920s. Botanicals are arranged there on four trays and slowly infused in the vapour before being condensed back to spirit.

This somewhat resembles the Carterhead process, in that it relies on the vapours passing over the key botanicals in order to create the desired flavour. The package is a most attractive one, with much emphasis on the number five: five sides; five Celtic botanicals; a five-pointed asterisk decorating the bottle; and so on. Caorunn thus proudly style themselves a 'small-batch Scottish gin' and bottle at 41.8% abv. Though technically this could be described as London Dry, it's a measure of the owner's self-assurance and confidence in the Scottish heritage that this takes pride of place on the packaging.

And why not? Great gin was always made in Scotland and Caorunn proudly uphold that tradition.

CITADELLE

Distillery:	Ferrand, Ars, France
Website:	www.citadellegin.com
Visitor Centre:	No
Strength:	44%

Citadelle is made in France, in the heart of the Cognac region, using direct-fired cognac stills. It was one of the first 'artisanal' distillers to produce gin, releasing the first batch of Citadelle in 1995 and the oak-aged 'yellow gin' Réserve in 2008.

Cognac distillers Ferrand are limited by law to producing brandy between November and March each year, meaning that the stills traditionally lie idle for six months of the year. That seemed a waste to company owner Alexandre Gabriel, so he decided to put his all-too-still stills to use by making gin in the months he could not produce cognac: 'I always loved the extreme complexity and the finesse that gin offered but was frustrated with what the market had to offer, which was usually too sharp for my taste. My dream was to produce gin with a capital "G" – Gin with some importance.'

So, he began to study the distillation methods used to make *genièvre* – the French ancestor of gin. With the help of a scholar, he rummaged through a century-old archive in Dunkirk where, amongst the crumbling papers, they found notes on ancient distillation methods to make gin (some as old as 250 years). A five-year battle to get the necessary permissions then ensued, but we can all be glad that M. Gabriel persisted.

Using nineteen different botanicals, infused for seventy-two hours, distilled for twelve hours using a small (twenty-hectolitre) hammered-copper pot still, and then rested before bottling at 44% Citadelle is a product of great subtlety and sophistication. As they explain: 'Few gins are produced in pot stills, and Citadelle is the only gin distilled in a cognac pot still with a naked flame. Distilling gin on an open flame requires a deft touch and far more attention than a column still or steam distillation which is otherwise used. It also means the gin is made in smaller batches, one cask at a time allowing the Master Distiller to precisely discard the "heads" and "tails" of the distillation, and only keep the precious, flavourful "heart" of the distillation.'

The oak-aged Réserve is particularly worthy of attention. Each annual batch is clearly dated and represents an evolution of the house style. It's a product made with great care, love and experience, reflected in a complex and rewarding taste that continues to satisfy and evolve to the bottom of the glass. Sipped neat, it is a revelation.

CITY OF LONDON

Distillery:	City of London Distillery, 22–24 Bride Lane, London
Website:	www.cityoflondondistillery.com
Visitor Centre:	COLD Bar
Strength:	41.3%

At the height of the Gin Craze (1720–51) it has been estimated that in parts of London one house in every four was a gin shop: this in addition to the countless hawkers selling gin on the street. In 1729, when the first Gin Act was passed, there were some 1,500 recorded distillers in London alone and, we may safely presume, any number of entirely clandestine operations.

So, our ancestors would not have been remotely surprised to step into a pub and find a distillery. That essentially describes the City of London Distillery, which is located in the COLD Bar on Bride Lane, just off Fleet Street. Stepping down to the basement bar comes as a total revelation to today's drinker. On the one hand is the bar, and directly opposite are the stills, nicknamed Jennifer, Clarissa and, most recently, Elizabeth to mark the Queen's ninetieth birthday.

They were first operational in December 2012, but the brand and distillery have since been acquired by the Halewood Artisanal Spirits group. Distilling and bottling of COLD gin and the Whitley Neill gins takes place here, making the bar a curiosity in its own right as the only manufacturing business in the City of London. I'm told that, as such, it attracts banking and finance types who creatively expense their visit as 'research into manufacturing industry'!

When I was a tiresomely ambitious young graduate, my first place of employment was not far from Bride Lane. I wondered aloud one day why the company's senior directors frequently retired at lunchtime and returned late in the afternoon rather 'tired and emotional'. In tones that brooked no further enquiry, I was told that they had 'been to a meeting' at the City Golf Club – in actual fact, the self-same licensed premises that today house the COLD distillery. Had it been there then, I doubt they would ever have returned to their desks.

The gin itself is a clean, crisp spirit with a pronounced citrus note – very tasty! At the COLD Bar you can take a tasting tour, make your own personal bottle by joining their gin school or just try one of the extended range of flavoured gins. Out of Six Bells Lemon Gin, Sloe Gin, The Square Mile Gin, Christopher Wren Gin, City of London Gin, Old Tom Gin, Rhubarb & Rose Gin, Murcian Orange Gin and Lime Gin there's surely one that appeals.

CONKER

Distillery:	Conker, Unit 3, 16a Inverleigh Road, Southbourne, Dorset
Website:	www.conkerspirit.co.uk
Visitor Centre:	Yes
Strength:	40%

Here's another one. Another bold pioneer prepared to abandon their chosen career, give up all those hopes and dreams, all those examinations, and chuck it all in to become a distiller. They must be bonkers! Or slightly nuts … Conker – get it?

In this case, our hero is former chartered surveyor Rupert Holloway, who, in setting up Dorset's first distillery, freely acknowledges that 'there's no ancient family recipe or mythical Master Distiller here, just a dogged pursuit of the new and exciting'. That's refreshing.

As he goes on to admit in his engaging blog, he's largely self-taught. Asked how he went from chartered surveyor to Head Distiller, he says, 'Anything can be learnt. So it appears that a lack of knowledge is no longer a barrier to entry. Pick any subject – no matter how complex or obscure – and you'll find everything you need from your phone. Today, your ability to become the expert in the room on practically any subject is restricted only by your tenacity to learn it (and perhaps your phone's battery life …).'

It only took forty-five recipe trials, though they went back to number thirty-eight after all that. Tenacity, you see. But in a little over six years, Conker has gone from strength to strength, expanded their range and opened a visitor centre, all while collecting some notable awards for their Dorset Dry gin. Dorset because of the fruity and herbaceous notes from the Dorset-inspired botanicals of elderberries, marsh samphire and handpicked gorse flowers. No horse chestnuts in there, though, which I'll admit did slightly surprise me, given the name.

However, I can't argue with the product. What we have here is good value for the small-batch distilling scene (about £36 for a full 70cl bottle), and it's bright and fresh without departing too far from a properly balanced juniper heart. The packaging stands out too as distinctive, with its cheery emphasis on Conker's 'That's the Spirit' line. There's also a Navy Strength with a donation to the RNLI, a Port Barrel-aged version and the frankly bizarre Mojito Gin, all from two 60-litre alembic pot stills named Pumpkin and Aunt Fanny.

They've been busy, thanks to Rupert the Conkeror! And as he now knows, gin distilling for the self-employed is far from the nine-to-five life of the chartered surveyor!

COTSWOLDS

Distillery:	Cotswolds Distillery, Stourton, Shipston-on-Stour
Website:	www.cotswoldsdistillery.com
Visitor Centre:	Yes
Strength:	46%

Here's a rather lovely distillery actually distilling in the heart of the Cotswolds in a charmingly bucolic setting we don't normally associate with industry.

The operation was established by former financier Daniel Szor. (Who says something good can't become of such people? Would that all bankers took up some small craft industry and got their hands dirty.) He saw the light some years ago, abandoning the City and following his dream of making whisky in the Cotswolds with locally grown and malted barley. Good idea, but tough on the cash flow, though the whisky is available now and proving deservedly popular.

But, while they waited, Cotswolds added gin to their line-up, using a bespoke top-quality German still – and very good it is too. Perhaps that's not surprising: they have actually gone to the lengths of employing a botanist to advise on locally grown botanicals.

The distinctive, non-standard botanicals include Cotswolds lavender and bay leaf, grapefruit and lime – everything goes into the pot and is distilled with the base spirit. The finished product is not chill-filtered. This may result in a slight cloudiness when ice is added, but it contributes to a smooth and rounded mouthfeel, which goes very well alongside the citrus and pine-juniper notes which are very much to the fore here.

It's a product that works well in a conventional G&T but is also a fine cocktail base – see the Cool Cocktails section for their variation on the English Garden made with their Wildflower style. That's just one of a number of different expressions they now offer as their creative distilling team explore the varied possibilities inherent in changing the botanicals. And, speaking of creative, while that's been going on, Dan Szor has had the temerity to write a book. As if the world needs more books ... oops!

The level of investment here – on distillery, offices and visitor centre, packaging, not to mention the youthful and enthusiastic team – speaks of a deep and lasting commitment by Szor, who claims not to have an 'exit strategy'. You might imagine at first glance that a call from a big distiller is hoped for, but I genuinely believe this isn't the case. It's illustrative of the fact that the craft-distilling sector is growing up very fast and, in its better exponents, producing distinctive and interesting products that add variety to our drinking repertoire.

CUCUMBER

Distillery:	The Langley Distillery, Langley Green, Warley, West Midlands
Website:	www.englishdrinkscompany.co.uk
Visitor Centre:	No
Strength:	40%

Oh dear! A cucumber-flavoured gin isn't exactly a new or ground-breaking idea. After all, Hendrick's was launched as long ago as 1999 (positively an eternity in gin years); Martin Miller's hints at it; Canada's Long Table Distillery offers us its take using cucumbers from British Columbia; and even good old Gordon's has raided the corporate cold frames to bring us their Crisp Cucumber.

What's more, there is no English Drinks Company distillery; like many others, they turn to a contract distiller to produce the liquid and concentrate their time and effort on actually selling the stuff. The thing is, though, it's actually rather good, and if what you're good at is sales and marketing, there is some sense in getting experts to make the product.

You do have to like cucumber, because this is very cucumbery. It reminds me of summer, of cricket teas, of lazy picnics by a meandering river – the essence of cucumber leaps from the bottle and demands to be finely sliced and placed, with infinite care, between two delicate, lightly buttered, almost transparent slices of crustless white bread, and eaten with an *insouciant* air. Yes, this is a very cucumbery gin, and your reaction to it will depend entirely upon your view of this humble comestible. After the cucumber there are some peppery notes and a bit of a juniper bite, but cucumber is the big star here. However, don't despair if this doesn't appeal, as they also offer Pink, Lemon, Orange and Lime variants.

But cucumber is not to be underrated: this versatile vegetable is noted for its contribution to healthy skin, relief from constipation, diabetes, kidney problems, acidity and sunburn, and as an antidote to bad breath. Pliny knew it to be a generally good thing.

Anyway, gin and cucumber has a long, if not illustrious, literary history. The unforgettable Sarah Gamp, the disreputable, dissolute nurse of Dickens' *Martin Chuzzlewit*, loved them: 'In case there should be such a thing as a cowcumber in the 'ouse, will you be so kind as bring it, for I'm rather partial to 'em, and they does a world of good in a sick room.'

Whether or not it works in gin I couldn't possibly say, but it must be worth trying.

DIPLÔME

Distillery:	Boudier, Dijon, France
Website:	www.diplomedrygin.com
Visitor Centre:	No
Strength:	44%

Did you know that the famous French scientist Professor Louis Pasteur started investigating the action of yeast on fermentation in a sugar-beet distillery in Lille in 1856? His work transformed the brewing and distilling industry, and is the basis of everything that we know today about fermentation (basically, for present purposes, turning a sugar solution into alcohol).

I mention this because the spirit base for Diplôme is made from beetroot (I assume sugar beet). That may sound odd, but in fact, if something contains sugar, you can ferment it, and a wide variety of sugars are found throughout nature. The yields will vary, of course, as will the flavour, but the end result will be a low-strength alcohol that can be distilled. Not many distillers today use a sugar beet base but then, as the French say, *chacun à son goût*.

I do not idly introduce this Gallic connection, for Diplôme is made in France – I note for your curiosity that neither the brand website nor the UK importer discloses the identity of the distiller, other than to say it is in Dijon. That is powerfully suggestive of Boudier, proprietors of their own Saffron gin, but, as no one will say definitively, this remains a speculation. I have no idea why they would wish to be so secretive, but there it is. I'm going to say Boudier until someone contradicts me.

What we are permitted to know is that the juniper berries, coriander, whole lemons, orange peel, angelica, saffron, iris root and fennel seed are infused in the spirit before being distilled in a pot still and eventually bottled at 44%. A fairly straightforward and old-school selection, then, with the notable exception of saffron, which again points to a circumstantial connection with Boudier. The simplicity of the recipe reflects the fact that this dates to the Second World War, when Diplôme was apparently the gin of choice of the US forces in Europe, hence the reference on the rather charming, typographically rich label (curiously similar to the Boudier house style) to the 'Original 1945 Recipe'.

Diplôme seems to have faded after the war and disappeared from the scene entirely until resurrected on the back of the current wave of enthusiasm for gins with authentic histories. It was relaunched as recently as 2013 but apparently already enjoys widespread worldwide distribution.

Beyond this, what I do not know I cannot tell. *C'est un mystère extraordinaire*. As they may or possibly may not say in France.

DOCKYARD

Distillery:	Copper Rivet Distillery, Pump House No. 5, Chatham Dockyard, Leviathan Way, Chatham
Website:	www.copperrivetdistillery.com
Visitor Centre:	Yes
Strength:	41.2%

Here we see the craft-distilling movement getting serious and really upping its game with a significant investment in premises, equipment and product development. The distillery is based in the magnificent Victorian Pump House No. 5 in the historic Chatham Dockyard, and located on the splendidly named Leviathan Way, where it has breathed new life into buildings which were abandoned in the mid-1980s when the dockyards were closed – something of an economic and emotional disaster for Chatham and the Medway.

Owned by the Russell family, who have links to the retail side of the drinks industry, Copper Rivet aims to reflect the engineering, innovation and entrepreneurship that once characterised this location. So, as well as refurbishing the impressive building (which they bought), they have worked with Master Distiller Abhi Banik, once of the prestigious Heriot-Watt International Centre of Brewing and Distilling in Edinburgh, to design their own unique gin still. Now that's bold – virtually everyone buys their stills from one of the established makers. Just to add to the frisson of uncertainty that must have accompanied that decision, they didn't take their design to a recognised stillmaker to have it built. They turned instead to a local business to fabricate this and Joyce, their own mighty column still where they make their high-strength neutral grain base. Fortunately, it's all turned out very well: not only did this underpin their local credentials but the smaller pot still – romantically named Janet – makes cracking gin.

It's their own exclusive recipe, naturally, developed after an exhaustive series of trials and consumer tests and, unusually, based on complete control of the entire process from grain to glass. Now that is painstaking and the sign of some true obsessives.

Dockyard gin is dry to taste, with an old-fashioned juniper and citrus note that will appeal to discriminating gin purists looking for complexity and great balance. All this is complemented by the slightly higher than normal strength and a striking presentation though I'd personally like to see a 70cl bottle being offered, having witnessed my neighbours polish off the contents of the current 50cl packaging before I could pour my own G&T. There's also a tasty Strawberry variant and I'm not sharing that with anyone.

'The Dockyard Spirit Endures' they say on the side of the bottle – well, not round here it didn't, but everything seems pleasingly shipshape at Copper Rivet.

DODD'S

Distillery:	British Honey Company, 32 Wornal Park, Worminghall
Website:	www.britishhoney.co.uk
Visitor Centre:	No
Strength:	49.9%

Poor old Ralph Dodd. This would-be entrepreneur, having failed in his dream to bore a tunnel under the River Thames, determined to start a distillery making Genuine British Spirits. Unfortunately, he omitted to complete the no doubt tedious legal formalities, fell foul of the 1720 Bubble Act, and in 1807 was obliged to drop his scheme without a drop ever being distilled. Notwithstanding his energy and entrepreneurial spirit, his patented building system and the construction of Britain's first underwater tunnel, he died a ruined man.

But, despite all that misfortune, in 2011 he was still remembered by the London Distillery Company (TLDC), which, in his honour, created a splendidly packaged gin with lots of engineering references on the label, and, I'm happy to say, a very fine product to which I'm sure old Ralph would have been happy to lend his name.

The company was created to be the first distiller of whisky in London since 1903, but, rather like the ill-fated Dodd, a number of rather unfortunate setbacks led to TLDC's collapse. The British Honey Company then acquired the Dodd's gin brand and transferred production to their site in Worminghall.

But the product remains true to the original recipe. Using its own proprietary method, not dissimilar to what Hendrick's does but on a rather smaller scale, a base spirit is distilled in a copper pot still. The organic ingredients, which are certified by the Soil Association, include juniper, angelica, fresh lime peel and British honey – which explains why they were interested to acquire the brand. Honey is unusual, but you really can taste the difference that it makes. A proportion of the base is then used to macerate more delicate botanicals such as bay laurel, cardamom and red raspberry leaf, and this is then distilled for a second time in a rotary evaporator or cold vacuum still. The two spirits are married for several weeks before being hand-bottled at 49.9% abv and labelled in small batches.

Bees, as you doubtless know, are very important to the ecosystem, so let's salute their gifts to the world with this delicious gin.

But to Ralph Dodd's prospectus for the launch of his ill-fated distillery business goes the last word: 'It is an evil too well known to require a dissertation – for the consequence arising from bad spirits, soon manifests in the destruction of its user.' He would know.

DOWNPOUR

Distillery:	North Uist Distillery Company, Nunton Steadings, Benbecula, Outer Hebrides
Website:	www.northuistdistillery.com
Visitor Centre:	Yes
Strength:	46%

If you head due west from Benbecula (it's an island in the Outer Hebrides, roughly on the same latitude as Hudson Bay in Canada), there's not a lot to see or do for rather more than 3,000 miles unless, of course, you like in-flight movies. The Atlantic Ocean comes between you and North America, and, as the prevailing winds cross the sea in the opposite direction to your plane, they pick up a lot of moisture which they drop – out of a malevolent sense of mischief, it seems to me – on the first land they find.

So, I was greatly amused that Jonny Ingledew and Kate Macdonald, two native Uibhistich (Gaelic for Uist folk), decided to call their island-inspired gin Downpour, with a striking but very simple label featuring a stylised rain storm that could feature on a contemporary Japanese print. And, just in case you missed the joke, the label reminds you that this is 'drenched in island flavour'. Someone has a very dry sense of humour.

This is a frontier sort of a place, known in Gaelic as the 'Dark Island', and not everyone is cut out for the life (I, for one, couldn't hack it though I love to visit these islands). There are few people and even fewer trees and, as I believe we've established, it rains quite a lot.

Eventually, they plan to distil a single malt whisky, using locally grown bere. That's the original barley used for Scotch whisky (Robert Burns celebrates it in his poem 'Scotch Drink'), but for the moment gin has got the fledgling business off the ground. Unlike many new boutique distilleries however, North Uist is in experienced hands as Jonny Ingledew has a background in brewing and distilling so can genuinely style himself Master Distiller.

He's wisely elected to deliver Downpour at 46%, aiming to preserve the essential oils from the botanicals and serve up a more intense mouthfeel. The gin may go cloudy when ice and a mixer is added, but that's a good sign of his commitment to quality and depth of flavour. Like the robust islanders, anaemic this is very definitely not.

Once in a while, they pick sloe berries and local brambles (like blackberries but with more och aye than the familiar commercial ones) to make a seasonal Sloe & Bramble Gin. This and other treats are available direct from the distillery where visitor facilities should open shortly after this is published.

EDINBURGH GIN

Distillery:	The Biscuit Factory Distillery, 4–6 Anderson Place, Leith, Edinburgh
Website:	www.edinburghgin.com
Visitor Centre:	Heads & Tails Bar, 1a Rutland Place, Edinburgh
Strength:	43%

Edinburgh Gin – it's made in Edinburgh in case you were wondering – could be held up as a case study for the craft-distilling movement. It was the brainchild of Alex and Jane Nicol, the husband-and-wife team behind Sheep Dip whisky. But Alex is a restless sort of chap and possessed of a fierce entrepreneurial drive – so much so that he was eventually able to sell the company to his distributors, Ian Macleod Distillers, who have the firepower to take this exciting brand to the next level of success.

To start at the beginning, back in 2010, observing the growing interest in gin, the Nicols determined to launch their own. But their inner entrepreneur has a streak of caution, so, rather than immediately open a small distillery, they had others make it. However, before long, sales grew to the point where a distillery could be considered. Once, Edinburgh had a flourishing distilling industry producing both gin and whisky – one eighteenth-century text claims that the city was home to more than 400 illicit stills, but that owes rather more to the overheated imagination of the partisan author (a fervent abolitionist) than any verifiable fact. What's certain is that gin distilling died out in Edinburgh when the Melrose-Drover distillery closed in 1974.

The Nicols re-established the tradition with a pub distillery at one end of Princes Street in a cosy basement bar, where you can see Flora and Caledonia, the stills, and book educational tours and tastings. It's so much more fun than the light industrial units that are home to some other small-batch producers, though, truth be told, they have another larger unit in Leith where most of the production takes place. Sadly, it's not open to the public, but here are plans for a splendid new distillery in the heart of Edinburgh's Old Town where all will be welcome.

With their Rhubarb variety, Edinburgh Gin was an early pioneer of flavoured gins and has gone on to develop an extensive range, as the distillery is constantly experimenting with new and different botanicals, either as full-strength gins or as liqueurs. Naturally, there's a Navy Strength version; first produced in the shadow of Edinburgh Castle, it's been named Cannonball, and 1670 is a handsomely packaged collaboration with Edinburgh's world-famous Royal Botanic Garden. A particular favourite of mine is their Seaside gin but the list goes on – just check out the website and prepare to be amazed.

ELEPHANT

Distillery:	Schwechower, near Hamburg, Germany
Website:	www.elephant-gin.com
Visitor Centre:	No
Strength:	45%

You must remember Babar the elephant, or Kipling's Elephant's Child and his "satiable curtiosity", or tales of Jumbo (late of London Zoo) and the great showman P. T. Barnum, or Mark Twain's 'Stolen White Elephant'. These gentle giants exercise a powerful hold on our imagination. Here in the 'civilised' West we deplore the wholesale slaughter of the African elephant to satisfy the apparently insatiable demand for ivory in Asia. Though you're probably feeling vaguely bad about that, few of us (and I'm as guilty as anyone) actually do very much about it.

But now you can! It's easy! Drink Elephant Gin (no elephants harmed in the making)!

Yes, company founders Robin and Tessa Gerlach and partners were so troubled by the 35,000 African elephants killed every year that they determined to help. After something of an epiphany on an African bush holiday they hit upon the idea of making Elephant Gin and contributing 15% of its profits to elephant conservation.

Soon Robin had to give up his day job in finance to concentrate on sales and marketing. Today, the product is distilled at the rather beautiful Schwechower distillery in Germany, where they make very fine fruit spirits, but the partners are actively looking to set up their own operation, probably using the current still. There are plans for a visitor centre – possibly opening in 2022. Check their website for news.

I must admit to a certain cynicism, assuming that the elephants were simply a marketing gimmick. I couldn't have been more wrong: while Gerlach can and does speak eloquently about his gin he moves to a different level when talking about elephants.

You probably care more about the unusual botanicals. They include baobab, the extraordinary buchu plant, devil's claw and African wormwood, sourced with the assistance of native African tribespeople. The botanicals also include mountain pine needles, specially cut in the Salzburger Mountains to complement the juniper. It comes in a custom bottle (50cl) with a splendid closure and handsome label – one of the best-dressed craft gins you can buy.

The range has been expanded and now includes the standard Dry Gin, the jumbo Elephant Strength (57%), a Sloe Gin and the most recent addition to the herd, Orange Cocoa Gin.

It's not cheap, but, all things considered, it is great value. Please don't forget that!

FARMER'S ORGANIC

Distillery:	United States Distilled Products, Princeton, Minnesota
Website:	www.farmersgin.com
Visitor Centre:	No
Strength:	46.7%

Another small-batch gin from the United States, Farmer's has the distinction of its organic status, which it announces proudly and prominently on the label. There are a few organic gins out there, but only a few, so if this is important to you, you'll have to do some searching. If you really care about such things, bear in mind that this organic certification comes from the USDA and is therefore subtly different from the UK's Soil Association. I'm not saying one is better than the other, just pointing it out.

Now, I'm not entirely convinced of the particular benefits of organic production to spirits. That's not to suggest that there aren't sound environmental and ethical reasons for organic production, it's simply a comment on the taste. But, after some consideration, that view probably comes from the dark spirits perspective, where wood maturation has a significant influence and the original spirit character is less evident. Clearly, that's not the case for gin, and here – whether due to organic production or not – we have a clean, fresh and very floral-tasting gin that stands up very well against its peers.

It's helped by the 46.7% abv strength. Not overpowering but with plenty of body, this means Farmer's excels as a cocktail ingredient and is not overwhelmed by even a good slug of ice and tonic. As an example of the 'New American Gin' style, the key point in the taste is that juniper has been dialled down (compared to, say, a British classic such as Beefeater), allowing other arguably more subtle botanicals to come to the fore.

Here we have elderflower and lemongrass that are evident on the palate, contributing to a less assertive but no less complex gin that I would expect to do well in blind tasting. In actual fact, it's recently collected a well-deserved Double Gold award from the San Francisco World Spirits Competition so its fame is clearly spreading.

The owners, Chatham Imports, who are linked to folks behind the highly respected Michter's family of American whiskeys, tell me that Farmer's comes from the United States Distilled Products (USDP) contract distillery in Princeton, Minnesota, which also produces their Crop Harvest Earth Organic vodka. USDP is not well known here, but you can be sure that whoever's distilling Farmer's knows what they're about, so let's hope they keep it up.

The secret lies in the soil, you know.

FOUR PILLARS

Distillery:	Four Pillars Distillery, 2a Lilydale Road, Healesville, Victoria, Australia
Website:	www.fourpillarsgin.com
Visitor Centre:	Yes
Strength:	41.8%

As you probably know, the Australians make some great wines. I can still recall a bottle of Yarra Yering Dry Red Wine No. 2 (prosaic title, stunning wine) that has me licking my lips at the memory. So they can probably manage to get something drinkable out of a still.

In actual fact, there is a vibrant Australian craft industry producing whisky that has surprised a few folks and some of the world's finest gins are to be found down under as well. One of the most exciting is Four Pillars in Victoria, self-proclaimed craft gin capital of the country. To be honest, I've lost count of the number of small distillers there.

Since running a highly successful crowd-funding campaign that meant their December 2013 first release sold out before it was made, Four Pillars have been striving to meet their aim 'to make the best craft spirits in Australia' – something which gets harder, such is the intensity of competition.

It began with the first new Christian Carl still in Australia, which they named Wilma after Head Distiller Cameron Mackenzie's late mother. Like his co-founders, Mackenzie comes from a wine background and believes strongly in the use of fresh fruit (he's not alone in this, but it is unusual). Having taken close to eighteen months to come up with the final gin, they use some unorthodox botanicals such as lemon myrtle and Tasmanian pepperberry leaf. Since then, distillery expansion has been good for the Christian Carl company as Four Pillars have bought four more stills, all named after various mums.

They are kept busy making an extensive range of gins that began with the original Rare Dry Gin and has grown with expressions such as Navy Strength (made with native Australian finger limes), Olive Leaf (olive oil and leaf), Bloody Shiraz (which involves steeping Yarra Valley Shiraz grapes in Rare Dry Gin) and a whole family of limited editions and collaborations using botanicals such as quandongs, macadamia nuts, anise myrtle and strawberry gum. And that's not to mention their love of barrel-ageing gins, including their annual release of Australian Christmas Gin, made by distilling Christmas puddings and ageing the gin in old muscat barrels.

All in all, it's no surprise that Four Pillars was named the International Wine and Spirits Competition's International Gin Producer of the Year in both 2019 and 2020. Fair dinkum, mate.

GARDEN SWIFT

Distillery:	Capreolus, The Mount, Park View, Stratton, Cirencester
Website:	www.capreolusdistillery.co.uk
Visitor Centre:	No
Strength:	47%

I'm not really sure that 'gin' does this justice, and having discovered Garden Swift (formerly Garden Tiger), I'm far from certain that I want to reveal much about it. My baser instincts tell me to keep this to myself, sharing a tiny glass with trusted friends after pouring from an unmarked bottle in case they track down their own supply and leave less for me.

Yes, it really is that good. Unfortunately for me, the Whisky Exchange got there first and made this their 'Spirit of the Year' in 2017 (incidentally, Nikka's Coffey Gin – see entry – took the crown the following year, so that's two gins in a row on a leading whisky retailer website, which tells you something about the current gin boom).

This is an incredible accolade. Capreolus had only been in operation for five months when selected. Out of all the spirits in the world – and some pretty stunning products had been chosen in previous years – a tiny Cotswolds distillery run by a remarkably single-minded individual, wildlife photographer turned distiller Barney Wilczak, came out on top. Swift or Tiger, this is a truly exceptional product, the result of an obsessive attention to detail: the glass is highly UV-resistant (top tip: dark glass bottles are better for your gin and often indicate a product made with especial care); the corks are very tactile; and the labels – letterpress-printed, naturally – are small works of art.

All this tender loving care heightens your expectations of the product, and you will not be disappointed. Wilczak has gone to immense pains in creating this elixir, an extraordinarily complex and satisfying spirit that will make you rethink everything you thought you knew about gin and how you drink it. This is not just a London Dry but, as Wilczak explains, 'a very complex but integrated spirit that shares the intricacy … in eaux de vie'.

With thirty-four botanicals – a combination of home-grown, wild and traded – this is probably the most multifaceted gin currently distilled in the UK, but it would be a mistake to focus on the absolute number, the result of a vast amount of detailed testing and rigorous selection. I could go on, but suggest you visit the website to get the full story.

You can serve this as a G&T or the recommended Chamois cocktail but personally I sip it very slowly, neat and unchilled from a tiny Georgian gin glass, reflecting on the love that has gone into making it.

GENEROUS

Distillery:	Cognac, France
Website:	www.generousgin.com
Visitor Centre:	No
Strength:	44%

The fantastically attractive-looking bottle had me seduced even before I broke the seal. This, I prophesy, will be one of the future successes of the craft-distilling movement, with the potential for significant growth – provided, of course, that they can manage the necessary increase in production while maintaining quality.

That's not easy. The challenges facing a small company in gearing up production to meet demand are significant. Finding the right people can be difficult, not to mention financing the growth itself.

But that's all in the future. Right now, it's time to enjoy a superbly produced gin from France that looks, feels and tastes like a potential world-beater. The company is small, relatively new and little known, but from their base in the Cognac region they have been producing a new French single malt whisky called Cortoisie and have also launched their Island Signature collection of rums.

I have to mention the packaging again. It's white glass with a beautiful tree-of-life design fired into the surface of the bottle. The shape fits wonderfully well into your hand and it's immensely satisfying just to handle and cradle the bottle before pouring. I suspect very few of these will end up in the recycling; they'll stay as decoration or be repurposed into lamp stands or even as vases for dried flowers. They're simply too attractive to throw away.

The attention to detail in the packaging alerts you to the fact that this is going to be something special, and the gin itself does not disappoint. I believe any gin distiller anywhere in the world would be proud of this. It's a 44% abv spirit so has a rich, zesty mouthfeel and a long-lasting consistent finish. Generous by name and generous in its nature, there is a lot to savour here. I loved the citrus notes, balanced by floral aromas but with plenty of underlying juniper to endorse the gin credentials and please the purist.

If you sip it neat, you'll pick out elderflower (always a great component in gin) and jasmine, but this works superbly well in a classic gin and tonic. You could try alternative garnishes such as grapefruit, satsuma or tangerine to draw out the citrus hints or go floral with a sprig of rosemary or some crushed elderflower leaves.

Just experiment. There are some great gins coming out of Cognac right now and Generous has really set a very high standard for their neighbours and rivals.

GIN MARE

Distillery:	Destilerías Miquel Guansé, Vilanova i la Geltrú, Spain
Website:	www.ginmare.com
Visitor Centre:	No
Strength:	42.7%

The words '*Mundus appellatur caelum, terra et mare*', Latin for 'the world is called heaven, earth and sea' (possibly a reference to the work of the seventh-century saint Isidore, Archbishop of Seville, whose collection of ancient texts greatly influenced the late medieval church), are to be found on a stained-glass window in a former chapel in the little seaside town of Vilanova i la Geltrú on Spain's Costa Dorada. So what? you may ask.

It also appears on the rather striking bottle of Gin Mare – Sea Gin – which today is made in said former chapel. Imagine, a chapel dedicated to gin with the still placed dramatically where the altar once stood – truly, they treat their gin with an almost religious devotion in Spain.

Since its launch in 2008, Gin Mare, soaked in all the influences of its Mediterranean home, has proved highly successful on the cocktail scene, though when partnered with its stablemate 1724 tonic, it also makes a stunning G&T – especially when served in the generous Spanish style. It is the creation of Marc and Manuel Giró, the fourth generation of a noted Spanish distilling house that is behind the popular GinMG and other brands. Their goal was to create a new contemporary, premium gin that reflected its origins.

To develop it, they exhaustively tested forty-five different botanicals, finally settling on a range that, along with wild juniper harvested from the family estate, included Arbequina olives (small, low-yielding and expensive), sweet and bitter oranges and lemons (all painstakingly hand-peeled), rosemary, thyme and basil, and more commonly seen gin botanicals such as coriander and cardamom. Hard though it is to credit, the fruit zests are macerated in neutral spirit for fully twelve months before it is deemed ready for distillation to begin.

That takes place in the distillery's custom-designed 250-litre Florentine pot still (interestingly a similar design is used in perfume manufacture and at G'Vine), after which the finished product is bottled, literally next door to the distillery, at 42.7%.

As might be expected from the unorthodox use of olives, rosemary and so on, this is a different-tasting gin – and one that, once tasted, won't be forgotten. Understandably, it's not the cheapest gin on the market but, with its unusual make-up and distinctive presentation, still offers excellent value.

If this is the sea, don't hesitate. Come right in, the water's lovely.

G'VINE
FLORAISON

Distillery:	Maison Villevert, Merpins, France
Website:	www.g-vine.com
Visitor Centre:	No
Strength:	40%

G'vine would like you to know five things about their gin. First, it's made in France from grape spirit. Second, and uniquely, it uses the grape flower as a botanical. Third, there are two styles: the lighter Floraison (40%) and the more traditional Nouaison (43.9%). Fourth, they make it in the Charente region of Cognac. That feels more like a refinement of number one, but we'll let them off. And, finally, it's distilled by Jean-Sébastien Robicquet, who created it back in 2005. Well, someone has to make it, so I think they're padding the list here: let's call it three things.

But G'Vine is no longer the only gin distilled using a grape-based spirit (Madrid's 'urban distillery' Santamanía does this, and so do Chilgrove in Chichester and the Menorcan Xoriguer). However, it was almost certainly the first new wave gin to do this, and it is genuinely unusual to find gin made in Cognac (though Citadelle are also there, using a more conventional wheat spirit).

Floraison is the more unusual and experimental of the two, more delicate and showing more of the influence of the grape flowers. Using them as a botanical really does seem to be unique, and it presents unique challenges: for one thing, there is only a window of around a fortnight in which they can be picked before they become small grapes, which is what Nature had planned for them all along.

After studying oenology, and then training as a lawyer, Jean-Sébastien worked in the international cognac trade before returning to the family vineyards. So, he brought the sensitivity of a trained winemaker to white spirits, observing that vodka and gin were growing far more rapidly than cognac and that their consumers were more open to innovation than the more traditionally orientated brandy drinker. It also didn't hurt that while cognac takes years to reach maturation, white spirits are ready much, much faster.

And so G'Vine was born. If you're not a very traditionally minded gin drinker you will probably prefer Floraison, whereas its partner the higher-strength limited release Nouaison will appeal more to the hard-core aficionado. The spicier, fuller flavour is influenced by a different balance of botanicals bringing the classic juniper and citrus notes to the fore.

Floraison, by contrast, may just be sufficiently subtle and delicate in flavour to become the gin to persuade vodka drinkers to try a grown-up drink.

HAYMANS LONDON DRY

Distillery:	Haymans, 8a Weir Road, Balham, London
Website:	www.haymansgin.com
Visitor Centre:	Yes
Strength:	41.2%

One could easily devote an entire book to Hayman's. Stand aside, newcomers! Here we have the fifth generation of a family of distillers – gin aristocracy if you will. If you visit their website or, better still, their splendidly compact distillery, you'll find they offer a wide variety of expressions including some really innovative products.

Their story starts in 1863 when the current chairman Christopher Hayman's great-grandfather James Burrough purchased a London gin rectifying business – their most famous brand then and now was Beefeater. Christopher joined in 1969 and was responsible for the distillation and production of Beefeater until 1987 when it was sold to Whitbread, then brewers (how things change – they stopped brewing in 2001 and today run a budget hotel chain).

But Whitbread and distilling didn't get on, and two years later, they sold their whisky and gin operations. The Haymans succeeded in buying up various parts of the business, and today Burrough's is owned by Pernod Ricard, who have done great things with Beefeater.

It just proves that you can't keep a true gin family down and soon they were distilling again, opening a permanent home in their splendid new distillery in Balham in March 2018, just four miles from the first 1863 distillery. There's a small visitor centre where you can see three operating stills and learn about the now rare two-day process they employ.

Their Old Tom, having been discontinued in the 1950s, was relaunched in November 2007 and is largely responsible for its revival. It's considered a reference point which defines the category, with a subtle sweetness derived as much from liquorice as the added sugar.

The standard bearer is their classic London Dry, which, since the move to Balham, has been subtly repackaged (very tasteful) and beefed up in strength. There are many London Dry gins but this is *primus inter pares* – the very quintessence of the style from a justly respected family company and Britain's senior gin dynasty.

But there's more, of which two are worthy of particular note. Small Gin (it comes in a 20cl bottle with a thimble to serve) offers lower alcohol and fewer calories with no reduction in taste and up to forty serves from one little bottle. It's witchcraft! And brand new as I write is their Exotic Citrus where kumquat, pomelo, Persian lime and mandarin have been added to their standard ten botanicals to dial up some bright, fresh citrus flavours.

HELSINKI GIN

Distillery:	The Helsinki Distilling Company, Työpajankatu 2a R3, 00580 Helsinki, Finland
Website:	www.hdco.fi
Visitor Centre:	Yes
Strength:	47%

Two Finns and an Irishman walked into a bar … No, that's not quite right. These two Finns and the Irishman actually *built* their own very funky bar in Teurastamo, which is an up-and-coming district of Helsinki – think Shoreditch and you'll get the general idea.

But, very sensibly, there's now a bar on top of Helsinki Distilling Company's very own distillery where this energetic and talented team (minus the departed Irishman) make some of the very nicest rye whiskey that it's been my pleasure to taste in a long time, aquavit, applejack, gin and distinctively Finnish gin liqueurs, and a thing called Helsinki Tyrnipontikka. I don't know what this is, but having tasted it, I'm happy to report it's just fine. Still can't pronounce it, though.

There's been an explosion of new craft distilleries in Finland (for example Kyrö and Teerenpeli) which have learned their trade very quickly and are producing impressive products. This Helsinki Gin was the team's first release and it's gaining them important awards and new fans in a number of markets.

It took a lot of determination to get the necessary permits and, in fact, this is Helsinki's first distillery in more than a century as the Finns explored their curious relationship with alcohol. Finnish has lots of drinking words – my favourite is *kalsarikännit*, which means to get drunk at home in your underpants, with no intention of doing anything else. They could almost be honorary Scots.

Nine hand-picked botanicals are blended with the purest Finnish water in the making of Helsinki Dry Gin. The unique taste, suggestive of the aromas of the Nordic forest with floral and citrus overtones, comes from Finnish lingonberries, rich Balkan juniper and Seville orange and lemon peels. Also found there are fennel and coriander seeds, orris root, angelica root and a small but important pinch of rose petals, resulting in a full-bodied and balanced gin. It is bottled without chill filtration so be aware that it may go a little hazy when served and, as the strength is a beefy 47%, note that you may go a little hazy as well once you have been served. Two large ones should just about do it. After that it's underpants time.

Their amiable Master Distiller Mikko Mykkänen puts his name on every bottle of Helsinki Gin. So would I, if I made it.

HENDRICK'S

Distillery:	Girvan, Ayrshire
Website:	www.hendricksgin.com
Visitor Centre:	The Gin Palace – trade only, by invitation
Strength:	41.4%

Hard though it is to believe, Hendrick's has only been with us since 1999, and wasn't launched in the UK until 2003, but the apothecary-style bottle and ingenious faux-Victorian marketing are suggestive of something much older: the get-up has fooled at least one gin 'writer' into describing it as 'classic'. It's anything but.

As the website and promotional material insist, this is a quite unusual product, something entirely in character for William Grant & Sons (think Glenfiddich and The Balvenie amongst others), who remain family-owned and determinedly independent. Since 1887, the company has followed its own path. Hendrick's is no exception: perhaps only Grant's would have named this brand after a senior family member's gardener who tended the roses key to the distinctive taste.

The distilling process is unusual: Hendrick's uses a blend of spirits produced from a 1948 Carterhead still and an 1860 vintage pot still. Both were bought at auction by the late Charles Grant Gordon, who built the original Girvan distillery to produce grain whisky. He appears to have purchased them on something of a whim, but later had them restored to working order. The two stills produce strikingly different styles of gin due to their different construction and methods of distillation, whereupon the two spirits are blended together and then essences of Bulgarian rose petals and cucumber are added (they are too delicate a flavour to be distilled with the other botanicals).

The brand was something of a sensation and, together with Bombay Sapphire, may be credited with transforming the market – there is no denying its immensely powerful influence in inspiring a new generation of boutique distillers. More recently, distiller Lesley Gracie has brought us limited editions, such as Midsummer Solstice, Hendrick's Lunar Gin and, exclusively in tax-free shops, Amazonia Gin, inspired by an expedition to the Venezuelan jungle. The Orbium expression is a permanent addition to the range.

I've always applauded its huge contribution to the category, had the greatest of respect for its astute and remarkably consistent marketing, and recognised that it's a very well-made product from a highly respected company, but previously I felt in two minds about Hendrick's, suggesting it was a trifle perfumed. However, now we're in a world where bacon and egg flavoured 'gin' can't be far off I've changed my mind – this is nothing short of a classic standard bearer for proper gin.

HERNÖ

Distillery:	Hernö, Dala 152, Härnösand, Sweden
Website:	www.hernogin.com
Visitor Centre:	Yes
Strength:	40.5%

pparently, this is a 'Swedish gin miracle'. Big claim, so let's find out more. The company was founded by Jon Hillgren, who was working in London as a bartender when he discovered gin (it wasn't lost – it's just that he didn't know much about it then). Much experimentation and many trials later, Jon founded Hernö Gin Distillery in 2011, which proudly claims to be Sweden's first dedicated gin distillery and the world's northernmost (as we go to print, but on current trends it won't be long before someone starts distilling at the North Pole).

The distillery is home to Kierstin, a 250-litre Holstein copper still, first installed in May 2012; since then they have expanded with two further 1,000-litre companions.

I'm not entirely surprised that it does well in competitions, where more forceful and strongly flavoured products can stand out in an extended tasting. The Swedish Excellence standard product is certainly an assertive, hot and spicy liquid, which initially drinks stronger than its 40.5% abv. I can see how it might cut through jaded palates, but when I first wrote about this, I worried that the majority of its really big medals had come from a trade magazine competition.

Well, that was then. Since my earlier gin book Hernö has gone on to collect significant plaudits. In fact, all the Hernö variants have been recognised, leading the brand's website to claim that since 2015 Hernö Gin is 'the world's most awarded gin distillery in the five biggest and most influential international competitions in the world'. Let's take their word for it as I haven't the strength to check!

So, if you like bold flavours, you may well care for this. I think Jon Hillgren deserves a great deal of credit for creating a product that stands out from the mainstream and can generate an enthusiastic following of supporters. Doubtless, they will flock to the Hernö Gin Bar in Stockholm which opened in the summer of 2020 and, looking forward, the Hernö Gin Hotel in Härnösand, which is planned for 2023 – an important step in Hernö Gin's long-term plan to establish Sweden's High Coast as an international destination for gin experiences and gin making.

And, in a couple of pages, after a crafty detour to the hills and harbours of bonny Galloway, we'll move on to another Swedish gin …

HILLS & HARBOUR

Distillery:	Crafty Distillery, Wigtown Road, Newton Stewart, Dumfries and Galloway
Website:	www.craftydistillery.com
Visitor Centre:	Yes
Strength:	40%

One of the unforeseen consequences of the boom in craft distilleries has been an implied questioning of the myth of the Master Distiller. The marketing gurus of the drinks industry had been keen to promote this idea, turning their production colleagues into minor rock stars possessed of esoteric knowledge and ancient, arcane skills known only to a privileged elite. The Master Distiller was touted as a member of a shadowy and secretive cabal, and it must be admitted that the drinks-writing community were generally happy to go along with this whimsical notion.

But if anyone can set themselves up as a distiller and, with a little training and the right equipment, produce spirits that, in blind tasting, stand comparison with the established authorities, then where stands the Master Distiller of old? All sorts of people are turning their hand to distilling these days – former surveyors, ex-bankers, farmers, even graphic designers – and making excellent, tasty products. Sometimes the product is gin or whisky and sometimes it's tourism, because direct sales to interested visitors, especially in an area popular with holidaymakers, are an essential part of the business model. So 'experiences' must be offered as well as elixirs, and here we have both.

The Crafty Distillery is run by Graham Taylor who, for fifteen years, was a designer (a very good one, as I have cause to know) but swapped that profession for the long hours of craft distilling in his native Galloway. He seems happy, and so he should be, because inside the rather tastefully distinctive bottle (he was a designer after all), we encounter a rather distinctively tasteful gin. See what I did there?

Hills & Harbour reflects the secluded forests and coastlines of Galloway, and, to prove it, Graham sent me a bit of a tree. It was from the noble fir, needles of which join bladderwrack seaweed and nine other botanicals in their stills. They're also keen to point out that they make their own wheat-based spirit from local grain, something which marks them out as serious distillers – Scottish Gin Distillery of the Year, no less.

And now plans for their own whisky are well developed. Or, rather, under development, because the final taste will be shaped by the opinions and feedback from an extended tasting exercise conducted by supporters evaluating samples of this new Lowland single malt.

Perhaps we're all Master Distillers after all – now, that's crafty.

HVEN

Distillery:	Spirit of Hven Distillery, Backafallsbyn, Hven, Sweden
Website:	www.hven.com
Visitor Centre:	Yes
Strength:	40%

P ay attention, for this is going to get complex. Established in 2008 to create Swedish whisky, the Backafallsbyn distillery is Sweden's third-ever pot still distillery, part of a wider movement there to create artisanal spirits in what was traditionally a heavily regulated market, with stringent government controls. It's located on the tiny island of Hven, between Denmark and Sweden, in Öresund, which you can only reach by boat. With fewer than 350 inhabitants, think of something along the lines of Jura.

So far, so simple. But wait. Oak-aged gins are seen frequently enough these days, but Hven take the highly unusual step (it may even be unique) of ageing their spirit in oak *before* it is redistilled into gin. First, they make their own organic wheat-based spirit and then vat it for twenty-four hours with their botanicals.

After that, the spirit is filtered off and filled into American oak casks, where it matures for eighteen months. Then, into the tall Hven stills it goes – lots of extended copper contact and reflux going on there, I would guess, as the stills have unusually tall necks. All that sounds unusual enough, but the distillery then rests the chosen final cut for another three months in steel vats. And then, at which point even the most obsessive of us would have cried 'enough', they distil it again before reducing it to a bottling strength of 40% abv, but without carbon or chill filtration.

So this isn't a 'barrel-aged' gin, but it is extraordinarily smooth, full-flavoured and rich. The botanicals, including locally sourced juniper, comprise grains of paradise, citrus, aniseed, Guinea pepper, Sichuan pepper, calamus root, cardamom, cassia and Mauritian Bourbon vanilla (I did get a strong vanilla hit from this but assumed it was due to the pre-ageing in American wood).

The flavours really do pop out very distinctly and clearly, yet Hven manages to be beautifully balanced and integrated. What's more, despite that time-consuming production method and rather charming packaging, it's not absurdly expensive. UK websites offer this at around £33 for the 50cl bottle (equivalent to a little over £45 for a standard bottle). That's not cheap, but you'll want to sip and savour this most distinctive gin, which offers excellent value for the quality and presentation. There's also a 57.1% Navy Strength offering more bang for your buck – whatever floats your boat, really.

JAISALMER

Distillery:	Rampur Distillers, Uttar Pradesh, India
Website:	www.jaisalmergin.com
Visitor Centre:	Yes
Strength:	43%

According to their website, Jaisalmer (the place) 'is the setting of a million tales about a time when royalty merged with culture, beauty with opulence and life was a mere dip in the massive ocean of royalty'. Apart from the small problem that I haven't the slightest idea what that actually means, I have to concede it sounds fantastic.

Anyway, Jaisalmer, the place, which is in Rajasthan in the west of India lends its name to this Indian craft gin, and as India and the story of gin are inextricably intertwined (at least for the British), I thought one Indian gin was called for. India is, in fact, a huge spirits market with some very large domestic producers. Most of their output, however, is regarded as rum in the West, though some very good true single malt whiskies have found their way here in recent years.

Jaisalmer, which is establishing a foothold here, is produced by Radico Khaitan, the people behind Rampur Indian single malt. Once you know that, expectations are raised, because this is one of the more progressive of Indian distilleries and their whisky has built a firm following amongst enthusiasts looking for a combination of quality and value.

It promises an Indian twist (a tonic, you might say) on classic gins with the hand-picked botanicals largely sourced there. Some eleven are used in the distillation, seven of which come from India itself. Coriander and vetiver, a spice with intriguing, complex peppery notes rarely used in gin, are grown in the fields around Jaisalmer while the sweet orange peel which complements the citrus and floral tones comes from central India. Cubeb berries and lemongrass are from the south, while the Darjeeling green tea leaves hail from eastern India and lemon peel from the west. Angelica roots, liquorice and caraway seeds make up the list.

So, what we have here is an Indian take on an English style of gin, and perfectly well done at that, yet it doesn't, at least to me, come across as especially, distinctively Indian. In writing that, I acknowledge the vagueness inherent in that piece of pomposity, but there are a few smaller brands from the region such as Greater Than, Hapusa, Love Delhi and Colombo No. 7 (from Sri Lanka) that offer a more exotic taste of the subcontinent – if that is your pleasure.

JAWBOX

Distillery:	The Echlinville Distillery, Echlinville House, 62 Gransha Road, Newtownards, Northern Ireland
Website:	www.jawboxgin.com
Visitor Centre:	Yes
Strength:	43%

I detect the hand of marketing here. From the elaborate Victorian-style labelling to the artfully crafted story, the brand manager has worked tirelessly to deliver all the right 'touch points', which have been carefully considered to reflect brand messages –all 'graft and craft', if I might borrow one of their favourite lines.

Not that marketing is a bad thing. It paid my mortgage for long enough, and this Jawbox does have a certain charm, not that it's going to let you forget it. The name, we are told, comes from the colloquial term for a Belfast sink and there's some rather romanticised 'good old days' copy on the label about the craic to be had around that hard-working porcelain.

The gin is also described as 'Belfast Cut'. Seeing as there hasn't, until very recently, been any distilling in Belfast since before the Second World War (and that of whiskey), perhaps the copywriter got a trifle carried away there, considering that this hails from the Echlinville Distillery, which is in Newtownards, some twenty miles or so from the city centre.

But mystery solved: the term nods to Belfast man Gerry White, the founder, with his thirty-odd years of drinks industry expertise, though several other parties have evidently joined in. Once past the surface blarney, there is a classic London Dry gin to be found: eleven botanicals, including local Black Mountain heather, all play their part in a big and bold, spicy and juniper-forward 43% spirit that makes a great G&T or cocktail base. The suggested serve is with ginger ale, which was apparently first invented in Belfast by one Thomas Cantrell, an apothecary, though today more closely associated with Canada.

There has been some significant investment in distilling plant and warehousing at Echlinville, which, when it opened in 2013, was Northern Ireland's first licensed distillery in over 125 years. The shiny new stills are housed in an impressive glazed stillhouse, and just one glance at the operation makes it clear that a free hand with the chequebook was required. Amongst other things, the old Dunville's whiskey brand has been revived here, and, if you were of a flippant turn of mind, you might be tempted to say they've thrown the kitchen sink at the distillery … sorry.

The thing is, it's hard to ignore the value on offer. You should find Jawbox relatively easily at under £30, and for some decent small-batch production that's not to be sniffed at.

JUNIPERO

Distillery:	Hotaling & Co. Distillery, San Francisco, California, USA
Website:	www.juniperogin.com
Visitor Centre:	No
Strength:	49.3%

Previously known as the Old Potrero Distillery, Hotaling represents a very interesting phenomenon: a business in transition from a somewhat quirky craft-brewing and distilling operation, very much the creation of one driven individual, to a larger, more corporate organisation. Junipero, one of the pioneers of small-batch gins, helped it get there.

It emerged from Anchor Brewing – a San Francisco craft brewer when the term was almost unknown – that had been saved from closure by Fritz Maytag, scion of a well-known domestic appliance company. Presumably, brewing looked more fun than washing machines. Having got the brewery back on its feet, for some time prior to 1993 he had been toying with the idea of making rye whiskey, which had been almost forgotten as a style. Making it in a pot still, then a revolutionary concept, worked well and led the team to further experimentation and exploration of distilling's history. From that apparently endless process, it was but a small step to gin, from which thinking emerged Junipero, arguably the USA's first craft gin, launched in April 1996.

Given the name, you don't need me to tell you that it's a very juniper-led gin. At the time, the idea of launching a pot-still-distilled craft gin was radical enough without wild experimentation in unusual botanicals. The gin revolution as we now know it was yet to kick off; this lit the fuse but stayed within well-recognised boundaries. The idea was not to break the rules but to create a well-crafted product on an unusual production basis. In that, Anchor succeeded, perhaps more fully than they could ever have anticipated.

At 49.3%, Junipero is a forceful character, well suited, like so many American craft gins, to mixing in a cocktail. Twelve botanicals are all worked together in the original, small copper pot still – the exact mix is undisclosed but one can detect a pronounced citrus impact, as well as the influence of coriander and what I take to be liquorice – but this is all about the juniper.

Maytag retired from the business in 2010, and after various changes of ownership, the company has more than tripled in size. Today, the distillery company is known as Hotaling & Co. after the turn-of-the-twentieth-century spirits dealer A. P. Hotaling. Refreshingly, though, they stay true to Maytag's original vision, making Junipero and no other gins under this label. The Original and Genuine, one might say.

KI NO BI
KYOTO DRY

Distillery:	Kyoto Distillery, Kisshoin, Minami-ku, Kyoto, Japan
Website:	www.kyotodistillery.jp
Visitor Centre:	Brand house at House of KI NO BI, Kyoto
Strength:	45.7%

This is – remarkably – Japan's first artisan gin distillery and is said to be the first distillery ever operated in historic Kyoto. That's remarkable enough, but what is really exceptional is that the Kyoto distillery was founded by a British team, Marcin Miller and David Croll, who, with David's wife Noriko, have now partnered with Pernod Ricard to achieve global distribution.

Everything about it reflects their love and respect for Japanese life and culture: their young distiller Alex Davies may have lived and worked in England until immersing himself in Japan, but Ki No Bi's distinctive glass bottles are handmade by craftspeople in Osaka's Sakai district and the screenprinted label – an elegant floral design displaying the gin's name, which means 'beauty of the seasons', in Japanese characters and Roman letters – is a collaboration with Kira Karacho. Founded in 1624, the company is Kyoto's oldest maker of karakami – paper printed with woodblock patterns.

With no tradition of gin distilling in Japan, stills were imported from Germany but the key ingredients are distinctively Japanese. Unusually, the neutral base spirit is made from rice and, apart from imported juniper and orris, the botanicals are sourced from in and around Kyoto. Juniper leads, of course, for this is a proper dry gin but ginger, bamboo leaves, red shiso, lemon and yuzu peel, sansho pepper, kinome leaves, Gyokuro green tea and hinoki wood emphasise the Japanese heritage. Ki No Bi's eleven botanicals are separated into six different flavour-led categories known as the Six Elements – Base, Citrus, Tea, Herbal, Spice and Fruity & Floral – and then macerated before being distilled separately and blending prior to the final marrying stage.

While gin may not have been distilled previously in Japan, it was not unknown. Ki No Bi was rapidly taken up by the famously demanding Tokyo mixologists. A Navy Strength style and a number of further limited editions have followed. Such was its success that initial supplies were limited, but you will now find bottles in the better specialists. It's not cheap, of course, but this is an exceptional product from a deeply committed team.

And it seems to have started a trend. This may have been Japan's first gin, but the country's two much larger competitors soon launched their own expressions (and very good they are too). Coincidence? Well, good timing certainly, and testimony to the thought and planning that characterises every aspect of this impressive operation.

KINTYRE

Distillery:	Beinn an Tuirc Distillers, Torrisdale Castle Estate, Kintyre
Website:	www.kintyregin.com
Visitor Centre:	Yes
Strength:	43%

Torrisdale Castle is on the Kintyre peninsula, between the splendidly named Grogport and Campbeltown, once a major centre for the distilling of Scotch whisky. It's a rather lovely part of Scotland, not least because it isn't heavily visited by tourists – though I daresay the castle would like a few more for their self-catering cottages (the servants' quarters look nice). The 1,200-acre estate remains in family hands. Once there would have been servants, lots of them, but today properties like this have to be self-sustaining and the Macalister Hall family have been ingenious in making the estate relevant to the twenty-first century, even if the lady of the house has to clean the holiday lets.

Torrisdale now features a bio-mass heating system fuelled by wood from the grounds, a hydroelectric scheme (it rains a lot on Kintyre) and, most recently, a gin distillery complete with gin school and café. Beinn an Tuirc – it means the Hill of the Wild Boar – proudly describe themselves as 'sustainable distillers', based on the fact that they generate their own electricity, use local spring water and two of their own botanicals, and, for every case of gin sold, plant a tree on the estate (which, in years to come, will doubtless be chopped down to feed the bio-mass boiler). A percentage of profits will support community projects and local business start-ups through a planned charitable foundation, which is only fair. After all, our taxes helped to build the distillery through the grant-making largesse of Highlands and Islands Enterprise.

So, that's a tick in all the right boxes, but is the gin actually any good? Well, they have all the proper kit (a smart, purpose-built German rig named Big Don after a late family member) and a recipe developed with help from the team behind Harris Gin. Add these credentials to the unique estate-grown botanicals (Icelandic moss and sheep sorrel), throw in some smart packaging (another family member owns a design agency) and a great story, and it almost doesn't matter.

But, fortunately, I can report that it's a well-made and full-flavoured offering with an excellently balanced nose and creamy mouthfeel. It has a long and agreeably spicy finish and, to its credit, avoids some of the more outlandish flavour notes that characterise some of the new small-batch producers. It performs well in a classic G&T, having enough weight not to be swamped by the mixer, and at 43% is a great cocktail base. Not boring at all.

LAKES

Distillery:	The Lakes Distillery, Bassenthwaite, Cumbria
Website:	www.lakesdistillery.com
Visitor Centre:	Yes
Strength:	46%

Lakes is a relatively new distillery, having opened in November 2014. It's based in and around some charming nineteenth-century farm buildings and seems to fit very naturally and comfortably into its landscape. MD and founder Paul Currie has family connections with the Arran Distillery in Scotland (they make whisky there, of course) and has recruited some serious well-qualified whisky distilling talent to run the operation here. It appears that they know a thing or two about making gin as well. Lakes is a slightly sweet drop that uses local botanicals such as bilberry, heather and meadowsweet to create a gin that is both smooth and engagingly complex. Juniper is ever present, naturally, but in this case it's locally sourced from the surrounding fells, and water comes from the River Derwent, so this is as artisanal and local as you get.

With the considerable Lake District tourist trade to boost their visitor numbers, all of them no doubt anxious to take home a souvenir rather more appealing than a copy of De Quincey's *Recollections*, the distillery's fame should spread far and wide, as those happy tourists float on high o'er vale and hill.

Since the launch, distiller Dhavall Gandhi has increased the strength of the gin to 46% from the original 43.7% but has maintained a minimalist approach to the number of botanicals (steeped overnight for gentle flavour extraction), believing that less is more in achieving a classic juniper-led profile. Always a sophisticated, balanced and utterly convincing product that can hold its head up in any company; it's got plenty of mouthfeel, weight and body, and shows convincingly how far the new wave of distillers has advanced.

The range has also increased to include two gin liqueurs and a second gin, which has replaced the previous Explorer style. This delicately blushing Pink Grapefruit style packs loads of citrus-forward notes, once again delivered at 46%. They suggest that it's served without a garnish, which, as we're all so familiar with the visual appeal of a slice of fruit, initially feels rather odd. But you can't always rely on getting pink grapefruit and, to be honest, it's a bit of a faff.

Another innovation is the stylish dedicated bottle, a handsome thing that could happily be seen in the smartest of chic nightclubs.

LANGLEY'S
NO. 8

Distillery:	The Langley Distillery, Langley Green, Warley, West Midlands
Website:	www.langleysgin.com
Visitor Centre:	No
Strength:	41.7%

Langley's Distillery was founded almost a century ago by the Palmer family and, since 1920, they have been developing and producing some of the finest award-winning gins in the world, now including their own. In fact, quite a number of gins start life in the West Midlands, in much the same way as happens with Thames Distillers. It's a substantial operation, with six stills, and, though arguably less famous than Thames, is equally well regarded by those in the know.

But, as this carries the distillery's own name, you'd be forgiven for thinking it was their own brand. Not so: it's another contract-distilled gin, this time for the Charter Brands company who wanted a gin for gentlemen, their theory being that many recently launched gins were too girly. That's not quite how they put it, but you get the idea – and you can make your own mind up. The 'No. 8' tag came about because eight botanicals are used and the eighth was the winning sample in their development trials, prior to the 2013 launch. It's made in Connie, a 4,000-litre English copper pot still from 1960 by John Dore & Co. that wouldn't seem out of place in a single malt whisky distillery. Incidentally, founded back in the 1830s, they are said to be the oldest pot-still producers in the world. Unusually, the botanicals aren't steeped in the neutral grain spirit prior to distillation but placed directly in the still immediately prior to firing (men, eh, they just can't wait – gotta rush into everything).

The high-strength gin then leaves Warley for Witham in Essex where it is bottled at 41.7%. While researching all this, I happened to note the curious coincidence that both Warley and Witham are mentioned in the Domesday Book. I don't suppose that's of the slightest significance, but it just struck me as curious and interesting. There's no charge – don't mention it.

What we can't avoid mentioning, though, is the 'gin for men' theory. Mark Dawkins, one of the men behind Charter Brands, has been so bold as to suggest that men have 'less of a sweet palate' and instead look for 'big flavours, complexity and a sophisticated flavour profile'. So, my wife being a total poppet, I thought I'd ask her.

'Interesting,' she said, 'but I don't want any more.' So there we have it: conclusive proof that my wife is definitely a woman.

LUSSA

Distillery:	The Stables, Ardlussa, Isle of Jura
Website:	www.lussagin.com
Visitor Centre:	Visits by appointment only
Strength:	42%

Once upon a time, I nearly visited the Lussa Distillery. Don't mock, because this is a most un-get-at-able place. That's what George Orwell said when he escaped here after the Second World War to write *1984*, and he was right. It's quicker and cheaper to fly to New York.

But then, like me, you wouldn't get to see this distillery in a stable and meet the three lady adventurers behind Lussa. I did get within twenty miles, though I was actually on Jura to write about whisky and learnt of the gin, which had only just been launched, quite by accident. Unfortunately, there was no time to make the return trip on the challenging single-track road and still make it back for the ferry.

Jura is a funny old place, famously home to one road, 250 people, 6,000 red deer and an Australian multi-millionaire who built a private golf course at a reputed cost of £55 million (you can stay there, but if you have to ask the price …). Much of the land is given over to deer forests, and the island is split into a few very large sporting estates held by rich absentee landlords. One estate, however, to the north end of the island is owned by the Fletcher family, who are the only owners in permanent residence.

Anyhow, Claire Fletcher, who originally came here to shoot a video for the KLF (their relationship with Jura is altogether another story) and stayed, has joined forces with two neighbours, Georgina Kitching and Alicia Macinnes. With a natty little Portuguese still to feed, they grow, gather and distil local botanicals that make up their adventure in gin. They have planted juniper bushes, harvest pine needles and sea lettuce, and grow other botanicals, fifteen in all, in polytunnels and greenhouses around the island to create a full-bodied and earthy gin with floral and citrus flavours. There are some lovely field notes on the website (which, let's face it, is probably as close as you're going to get).

However, if you do manage a trip to Jura – and it's something I'd definitely recommend – you can arrange a distillery tour with a bottle to take home. Living on an island, especially one as extreme as Jura, is not my idea of fun. It takes a very special personality to hack it, so to combine that with growing a business is quite admirable.

So, Claire and friends – respect! (They like it when I say that.)

MAKAR

Distillery:	Glasgow Distillery Company, Glasgow
Website:	www.glasgowdistillery.com
Visitor Centre:	No
Strength:	43%

The Glasgow Distillery Company, proud crafters of Glasgow's first legal gin, Makar Original Dry Gin, is backed by some serious and well-connected drinks industry personalities and is evidently well funded. If you doubt that, just take a look at the substantial investment in distilling capacity as well as the stylish customised bottle. High-quality design and bespoke glass moulds don't come cheap, so this is a big statement of intent from the producers behind Makar, the Scots term for a poet or bard. The venture, not to be confused with another rival Glasgow distillery which is located on the banks of the River Clyde, is located in Hillington Business Park to the west of the city. Apparently, a total investment of 'several million' pounds was involved.

The Glasgow Distillery is home to several premium spirit brands, not just their five-strong range of Makar Gin, including Glasgow 1770 Single Malt Scotch Whisky, Banditti Club Rum, Malt Riot Blended Malt and G52 Botanical Vodka.

Makar gin is produced in the distillery's 450-litre Christian Carl still, a pot still with a seven-plate column that has been christened Annie. The still alone is a £100,000 piece of equipment, capable of producing some 300 bottles from each seven-hour distillation run. You wouldn't commission this if you weren't pretty intent on making a big splash.

While whisky might be the first spirit that comes to mind, many fine gins are made in Scotland, and this Original Dry gin, plus the remaining four gins in the Makar range (Oak Aged, Mulberry Aged, Old Tom and Cherry) join that number. A traditionally styled gin, it's loaded with juniper berries and uses seven other botanicals: angelica root, rosemary, liquorice, black peppercorns, coriander seeds, cassia bark and lemon peel. The distinctive bottle certainly stands out on back bars, an increasingly important point of difference as the market for small-batch gins becomes ever more congested. The seven sides of the bottle are intended to represent the seven botanicals added to the juniper – and also make the bottle easy to grip and pour, which will no doubt be welcomed by harried bar staff.

Makar's taste is clearly, and very properly, described as 'juniper-led' – very markedly a world away from the lighter, more floral style of some new gins. Makar is bold, assertive and forceful – no mean gin, in fact.

MALFY CON LIMONE

Distillery:	Torino Distillati, via Montegrappa 37, Moncalieri, Turin, Italy
Website:	www.malfygin.com
Visitor Centre:	No
Strength:	41%

Developed originally by a US-based drinks agency, Malfy was bought in June 2019 by Pernod Ricard (owner of Beefeater, Plymouth, Ungava Monkey 47 and Ki No Bi Japanese gin) to complement their impressive portfolio of premium, small-batch gins.

Looking at that list, the world is evidently their oyster, but this takes us to Italy where Malfy is distilled by the Vergnano family in Moncalieri, using a stainless-steel vacuum still and unique Italian ingredients. They've been distilling there since 1906 but make the curious claim that eleventh-century monks on the Salerno coast added *ginepro* (juniper) and other botanicals to base alcohol and that, accordingly, gin began in Italy. I'm not sure that they buy that in Holland, but, frankly, who cares? This is nicer and very far removed from anything eleventh-century monks would cook up.

So, forget the Low Country, this all about the spirit of Italy and the Amalfi Coast. In this stylish, sun-soaked enclave, life moves at a different pace – according to the tourist board at any rate. I'm a sucker for citrus-led gins, hence featuring this expression rather than the others in the family. Tasted neat, it's quite robust, but this isn't one for thoughtful sipping – rather this screams of *la dolce vita*, or even *dolce far niente*, the sweet art of doing nothing …

I could see myself doing nothing with a glass or two of this on board a Riva Rivamare, speeding past Mr and Mrs Clooney's Villa Oleandra in Laglio on Lake Como and raising a glass to the locals. Or possibly in some chic bar in Portofino or Santa Margherita Ligure, people-watching and happily contemplating the imminent arrival of my dinner. It's a languorous, luxurious and indulgent drop that is very heavy on the lemons – perhaps some seafood is suggested?

As far as the gin itself is concerned, it's not overly complex, employing just six botanicals and a wheat-based alcohol which has been steeped in a blend of Sfusato Amalfi coastal lemons, lemon peel, pink grapefruit and oranges. The still is unusual, however; the principle at work being that the freshness and vitality of the citrus is preserved by low-temperature distillation. The result won't necessarily appeal to the juniper loyalists (who won't like the packaging either), but along with the more recent Rosa (Pink Grapefruit) variety, this is adding something fresh to the gin-drinking repertoire, even if the creation story upsets our Dutch friends.

MARTIN MILLER'S GIN

Distillery:	The Langley Distillery, Langley Green, Warley, West Midlands
Website:	www.martinmillersgin.com
Visitor Centre:	No
Strength:	40%

This highly awarded gin was one of the earliest premium gins, and has been notably successful since its launch in 1999. It's probably an inspiration to today's craft distillers hoping to emulate its apparently effortless rise to fame.

The eponymous Martin Miller was a true English eccentric – bon viveur, photographer, author, publisher of Miller's Antique Guides, hotel proprietor and probably half a dozen other things as well – who apparently came up with the idea for his gin in 1998, after finding that the gins then on the market fell short of his discriminating standards. So, he decided to create his own. As you do. Well, you do now, but back then things were different: this was quite a radical proposition.

Two things make this stand out: first, the distillation. It's not that Martin Miller's employs a huge number of botanicals or some arcane ingredient that no one has ever heard of; no, they simply split the process into two separate distillations. The juniper and the 'earthier' botanicals along with the dried lime peel are distilled first, then the citrus peels, combining both distillates later. This balances the signature notes of juniper and the bright, refreshing citrus notes. Not so unusual today, but unorthodox just twenty years ago. It does mean, however, that Martin Miller's doesn't qualify as a London gin.

The next step remains, I think, unique. The high-strength distillate is reduced to drinking strength with water from Iceland. It seems like a lot of trouble to go to (in fact, you might almost consider it a gimmick), but the company argues that, despite accounting for about 50–60% of the contents, normal demineralised water is 'dead'. According to the company, Icelandic spring water (they have their own spring now) is 'simply the purest and softest naturally occurring water to be found on the planet', which qualities make it perfect for blending gin. All this shipping water across the high seas might strike you as expensive and so you'd expect Martin Miller's to be pricey.

Actually, you can find it widely available under £30; not the cheapest, then, but hardly overpriced in a world of small brands looking for £40 plus. Lots more information is on their generally excellent website where, in tribute to their late proprietor, they have majored on a 'madness to genius' theme. I think he'd approve.

MISTY ISLE

Distillery:	Isle of Skye Distillers, Rathad na Slignich, Portree, Skye
Website:	www.isleofskyedistillers.com
Visitor Centre:	No. Shop and gin school
Strength:	41.5%

The 'Misty Isle' is Skye itself, named for the clouds which gather around the island's dramatic Black Cuillin mountain range. It does, as you probably realise, rain quite frequently here but, as they say, if you don't like the weather, all you have to do is wait, as something different will be along very soon.

In distilling terms, Skye is best known for the forceful single malt whisky distilled at Talisker and, more recently, its smaller rival Torabhaig. Neither make gin, but while Skye waited several hundred years for its first gin distillery, two came along curiously close together.

Skye's second gin is called Skye Gin, but as the Isle of Skye Distillers were the first to open (and as one of the two brothers behind this served in the Paras), it seemed appropriate to focus on their small distillery in Portree. (You can find the other guys at Uig if you're curious.) They offer quite a range: the original Misty Isle; Misty Isle Pink, an interesting take on the sweetened Old Tom style, featuring pear, blackcurrants and meadowsweet with infused raspberries, all harvested from the distillery garden; Misty Isle Cill Targhlain (the original Gaelic name for Portree – don't worry if you can't pronounce it); Spookily Spiced; Mulled Christmas Gin; and limited edition Tommy's and the Commando Gunners, both with military themes.

There's no visitor centre but owners Thomas and Alistair Wilson do run a gin school, offering the hands-on opportunity to learn about distilling while making your very own gin to your own exclusive recipe. With tourism an important part of the local economy, businesses such as the Isle of Skye Distillers add variety and fun to visitors' experience of the island. Not everyone wants, or is able, to tackle the demanding Cuillins, so it's important to have something to do when it's raining, which it undoubtedly will.

And here's a tip. If you plan to visit Skye – and you definitely should – be very sure that you have booked some accommodation, especially during the school holidays, even if it's a camping pitch. At peak seasons, Skye gets very, very busy. It's not unknown for ill-prepared visitors to the Crowded Isle to end up on a temporary camp bed somewhere, at which point gin is definitely required.

MONKEY 47

Distillery:	Zum Wilden Affen, Lossburg, Germany
Website:	www.monkey47.com
Visitor Centre:	Wild Monkey Distillery, Schaberhof, Germany
Strength:	47%

ere's something clearly put together by an obsessive. I mean that in a good way, because I really did love every 'touch point' – some marketing jargon there for you – about the brand even before I opened the really lovely bottle.

And then I positively squealed with pleasure … There is a little metal collar to the cork, and, squinting at it, you will find a Latin motto, *Ex pluribus unum*, which I take to mean 'out of many, one' – a reference presumably to the forty-seven different botanicals (including six different peppers – *six*, I mean, come on) that go into this uniquely German gin which, no surprise, is bottled at 47% abv. And, if you look even more closely, the metal is exquisitely engraved and delicate little crosses separate the text. You really have to be slightly mad to go to this trouble – and I love it.

You might think the bottle owes something to Hendrick's and the label to Elephant (or perhaps vice versa), but the product is unique. Obviously, every product is unique, but this is *really* different. Their website is a thing of joy, on which you can happily spend hours reading about monkey species, the jazz of Oscar Peterson, cork trees, Eddie the Eagle and many, many different cocktail recipes, as well as their history, various different botanicals and the origins of Monkey 47. Incredibly, it can be traced to the personal recipe of a British RAF officer, Wing Commander Montgomery Collins, who settled in the Black Forest in the 1950s with the aim of becoming a watchmaker.

Fortunately for us, he apparently wasn't very good at it, so he opened a guesthouse instead and named it the Wild Monkey in honour of Max, a monkey he had sponsored in Berlin Zoo immediately after the war (so, technically, a *captive* monkey). There, he attempted to recreate English gin, but with added local ingredients.

Thinking about all that, he must have been a true British eccentric. His spirit (pun intended) has been captured by founder Alexander Stein and his splendidly hirsute Master Distiller Christoph Keller, who, in recreating Collins' recipe, makes what wine critic Robert Parker called 'the greatest gin I have ever tasted'. Astonishingly, after distillation, the spirit rests for three months in earthenware crocks before it's reduced for bottling. Little wonder then that it's been voted Top Trending Gin in *Drinks International*'s Annual Brand Report five years running.

NB

Distillery:	NB Distillery, Halfland Barns, North Berwick, East Lothian
Website:	www.nbdistillery.com
Visitor Centre:	Yes
Strength:	42%

N.B. Nota bene. Latin for 'note well', the phrase first appeared in text around 1721. 'Pay attention' it says.

And if we were in Scotland, we might remember that Scotland once more or less happily referred to itself as NB, 'North Britain', hence the nomenclature of Edinburgh's grandest of grand railway hotels, the North British. Sadly, it has rebranded itself into the anodyne Balmoral Hotel. Which, as any Scot could tell you, ought by rights to be on Deeside, not in the heart of Auld Reekie.

NB also stands for North Berwick, a pleasant seaside town right on the Forth Estuary, about twenty-five miles east of Edinburgh and once a fashionable seaside resort. I have fond memories of North Berwick because in another life I played a role in establishing the town's principal attraction, the Scottish Seabird Centre.

And now it has something else: its very own distillery, a little one, with a John Dore still (not many of those about), making around one hundred litres per batch of NB Gin. It's a fairly straight-along-the-line London Dry gin, using just eight botanicals: juniper, coriander seed, angelica root, grains of paradise, lemon peel, cassia bark, cardamom and orris root. As you might expect, it's pretty much old-school in style (nothing wrong with that), with plenty of juniper and orange notes, and bottled at a sensible 42% abv.

The distillery is the brainchild of husband-and-wife team Steve and Viv Muir, who have taken a very hands-on role at their microdistillery, since launching it in October 2013. It's found a ready local acceptance and even made it into some export markets, despite the rather basic packaging. Oh, all right, it's minimalist, or retro or something – and it does come in a box, if you're concerned about that kind of thing.

I'd rate this a very decent cocktail gin. Apparently Charles Maxwell of Thames Distillers advised on the development tasting panel, which was pretty decent of him, and rated it 'a very fine gin that was extremely likeable'. He should know, if anybody does.

So, you see, NB does stand for 'pay attention' after all. Given a decent sea breeze behind it, we should see more of NB Gin.

NIKKA COFFEY

Distillery:	Miyagikyo Distillery, Miyagi-ken, Japan
Website:	www.nikka.com/eng/brands/coffey-gin-vodka
Visitor Centre:	Yes (Japanese-language only)
Strength:	47%

Not 'coffee' but Coffey, a nineteenth-century Irish Excise officer turned distiller who, in 1830, patented an improved design for a continuous still. There were other similar stills operating around this date, but Coffey's proved the best and stood the test of time. In fact, though his very first examples were made of wood, an original example is still running in Guyana where it makes rum.

Today, there are multi-column designs offering greater efficiency and producing a purer spirit. But the old two-column still, originally imported from Scotland more than fifty years ago, operated by Nikka at Miyagikyo produces a spirit with greater character and texture. Nikka is best known for its whiskies, and for most of that time the still has been employed by them to make the grain whisky they need for their blends. However, in 2012, the venerable old apparatus came out of the shadows with the release of an unusual single grain whisky which was quickly followed by their Coffey Gin.

Alongside the malt distillate, the Coffey still is also used to produce a rich and silky maize spirit, which on its own is the base used to infuse and distil the botanicals. These include Japanese citrus such as yuzu, kabosu, hirami lemon and amanatsu, a touch of apples and the tangy Japanese sansho pepper, with juniper in there as you would expect. However, in what seems to be emerging as a distinct style in Japanese gins, the botanicals are divided into three groups – sansho pepper, fruit and herbs/spices – and distilled separately. The herbs and spices are distilled in a regular pot still, but the citrus and pepper are distilled at low pressure to maintain more of their delicate flavours, with all five components finally blended prior to bottling.

The dominant note comes from the various citrus components, which make this fresh, fruity and very refreshing, though with plenty of weight due to the 47% bottling strength.

Perhaps not everyone will care for the strong citrus-forward nose and taste of this gin and the subsequent peppery notes, but if you want something a little out of the ordinary, something that will stand up to the inevitable dilution of a G&T or classic cocktail, then this could well be for you. One idea might be to get a bottle of this, Ki No Bi and Roku and serve them blind in a Japanese gin tasting.

OPIHR

Distillery:	G. & J. Distillers, Clayton Road, Warrington
Website:	www.opihr.com
Visitor Centre:	No
Strength:	40%

Right, before we get started on this distinctly quirky gin from Master Distiller Joanne Moore (a woman with a restless and inventive mind who is responsible for a number of interesting products), let's begin by saluting the marketing brain behind it all.

For surely this is a marketing creation: the get-up is very pleasing; both bottle and label design are deceptively simple (that takes a lot of skill); and the whole package has a tactile quality that's hard to resist. They call it 'shelf appeal' in the trade. Someone has then come up with a load of half-believable guff on the website and back label describing Opihr as 'a legendary region famed for its wealth and riches which prospered during the reign of King Solomon. The King regularly received cargoes of gold, silver and spices from Opihr and whilst its exact location remains a mystery, it is thought to have been in the Orient along the ancient Spice Route.' Well, I suppose since the whole thing is a legend it could as well have been in Timbuktu or darkest Neasden for that matter (possibly not Neasden). It's generally spelt Ophir; I haven't the slightest idea why they changed it.

Opihr – it's pronounced 'o-peer' by the way, though under the influence of H. Rider Haggard I still badly want to spell it Ophir – is apparently targeted at 24–35-year-olds with a sense of adventure. That rules me out. It's certainly not going to appeal to the Jaguar-driving golf-club member who could be considered the archetypal gin drinker (though I don't fit in there either). Whatever, as I have been told adventurous 24–35-year-olds might say.

Right there on the label, centre front, are the words 'Oriental Spiced'. So, the mighty hit of cardamom and pepper that envelops your nose as you open the bottle shouldn't come as a surprise, even if the idea of a spiced gin is mildly shocking. With its recent releases, brand owners Quintessential really are pushing at our understanding of what gin should be.

They've clearly done well with the spice route concept though, as Opihr now comes in four variants: Oriental Spiced (discussed above) as well as the European Aromatic Bitters, Arabian (Black Lemon) and Far East (Sichuan pepper) editions, all of which play flavour tunes with a variety of botanicals. It's an interesting and quite intriguing route to explore that might spice up your gin journey.

ORIGIN

Distillery:	The Orkney Distillery, Ayre Road, Kirkwall, Orkney
Website:	www.origin-gin.com
Visitor Centre:	Yes
Strength:	43%

Well, if you needed one, there are now at least three gin reasons to go to Orkney (as well as Highland Park and Scapa distilleries for great whisky) as gin seems to have taken over these lovely islands. There is the Orkney Gin Company and also the Deerness Distillery, but I'm awarding the crown to Origin (originally known as Kirkjuvagr) from Orkney Distilling, who are based in Kirkwall. Incidentally, Orkney is somewhere you should visit at least once in your life, but be warned, once you've been, you will want to go straight back.

It first began life at Strathearn in Perthshire, where they worked to develop the recipe and distil the initial batches, but very soon they opened a splendid purpose-built distillery and visitor centre in a smart new building right by Kirkwall harbour (it's no coincidence that the distillery's energetic founder Stephen Kemp and his wife Aly own a substantial construction company).

It's also no coincidence that the site is very close to the point where visitors from the many cruise ships that call into Orkney disembark. These behemoths can carry up to 5,000 passengers, more than half Kirkwall's population, all of them desperate for an insight into island life. And, if that can be accompanied by a tasty G&T, well, perhaps Skara Brae can wait.

But for all that, the product is deeply rooted in Orkney. The Kemps worked closely with the island's highly regarded Agronomy Institute and make extensive use of local botanicals, to the extent of incorporating some Orkney-grown bere (an early landrace strain of barley) in their gin. Early success meant that the distillery was soon expanded and capacity increased with two 200-litre Hoga stills from Portugal. The range has also grown to include Arkh-Angell (an impressive 57% Navy style), Aurora (a spiced style, marking the long, dark nights of an island winter) and Beyla, which is a honey- and raspberry-influenced Old Tom expression.

As is clear, the whole project was very much an Orkney effort, and it has enjoyed a good deal of local support, with graphics by a local designer, and Nicola Wylie, hailing from Kirkwall, looking after the distilling. Now in full production, Origin will be a welcome addition to our shelves here, always assuming that those thirsty cruise-ship passengers, latter-day Vikings, leave any for the rest of us to enjoy after pillaging the distillery shop.

OXFORD RYE ORGANIC

Distillery:	The Oxford Artisan Distillery, South Park, Cheney Lane, Oxford
Website:	www.theoxfordartisandistillery.com
Visitor Centre:	Yes
Strength:	43%

I must confess to some concern when I learned that the neophyte distillers behind Oxford's first-ever distillery (remarkable, but true it would seem) designed their own equipment. That twinge of apprehension only grew on hearing that they turned to a firm of railway engineers to help build their unorthodox stills, insisting that they incorporate an old ship's porthole into the design.

My brow was ever more deeply furrowed by their insistence on heritage grain, the knowledge that the distillery's founder lives on an old barge and that their first Master Distiller was self-taught in his own illegal speakeasy in a Brooklyn loft ... It all seemed too hipster steampunk to have terribly much credibility or longevity.

But they're still around! And since first writing about them, much has changed. In fairness, the stills do look amazing and work just as effectively. Their current Master Distiller Chico Rosa comes with great distilling credentials, and behind the self-conscious stance with its talk of sustainability, there is a seriousness of purpose, some real intellectual depth and a coherent philosophy. I guess that's what the folks at the Oxford Botanic Garden and the Ashmolean Museum saw when they were persuaded to lend their name to TOAD gins. Except, sadly, the distillery no longer uses the TOAD acronym – I was sorry to see that quirky detail disappear.

Since their first release of Oxford Dry Gin, the original version has evolved following organic certification by the Soil Association of the base spirit, which is distilled from ancient heritage grains, grown within fifty miles of Oxford. The range has expanded too: vodka, naturally; the first whisky has been released; and there is Cuisse de Nymphe, an intriguing, sweet gin liqueur which uses aromatic organic rose petals and apples, alongside Dam Sloe Gin made from wild damsons and sloes. It spends a year maturing on the Oxford Rye gin base, hence dam(n) slow ... groan. Don't blame me – it's their 'joke'.

But this distillery is, in some ways, more important than the products it makes. Their approach challenges current orthodoxy and insists that we can look at distilling holistically from grain to bottle. Setting up and running a small business is challenging enough and the life of a small-scale craft distiller isn't a bed of roses – to attempt it while defying industry norms requires either real courage or, more likely, a certain perversity of character and a wilful refusal to consider the stakes involved.

OXLEY

Distillery:	Oxley Spirits Company (Thames Distillers Ltd for Bacardi), Timbermill Distillery, Clapham, London
Website:	www.oxleygin.com
Visitor Centre:	Certainly not!
Strength:	47%

This rather beautifully packaged super-premium gin is actually a Bacardi product – not that you would know that from its low-profile approach. Once upon a time, I wanted to see it being made, so I asked to visit the distillery. Though I enquired politely enough, their PR guy recoiled in horror. 'That won't be possible.'

I like a challenge, so, just a few days later, I breezed nonchalantly onto a nondescript South London industrial estate sandwiched between a timber merchant and a railway, trying to be inconspicuous (those PR folk have spies everywhere). Having negotiated an intimidating security barrier, I found a large metal shed, with all the glamour of a run-down carpet warehouse.

But appearances are not everything, for here I saw the Oxley Cold Distillation process. The still – unrecognisable as such – appears to be something from the laboratory of *Back to the Future* inventor Emmett Brown. But from it flows slowly – excruciatingly slowly – a gin of sublime delicacy and refinement, so perfectly smooth, fresh, creamy and utterly mouth-watering that I have been known to sneak a good tumblerful, neat and at room temperature. Bad Ian.

Vacuum distillation is not entirely unknown, but Oxley have combined this with a gizmo that forces the spirit vapour to hit a cold thingy (I promised not to reveal the technical secrets). And by 'cold' I mean *cold*. Colder than penguins' feet. Colder than an unimaginably cold thing on Planet Cold.

This means that all the delicacy and freshness of the botanicals are retained, including, most unusually, fresh grapefruit, orange and lemon. When you uncork the bottle you get a delicious burst of enticing citrus notes entreating you to 'drink me, drink me'. Apparently they had thirty-eight goes at the recipe. They got it right, if you ask me.

What I don't think they got right – and I'm surprised – is the marketing. When launched in August 2009 it was ahead of the gin boom and the pricing around £50, albeit for a 1-litre bottle, was ambitious. So, it's never really enjoyed the visibility that I believe it should receive and, though praised by top bartenders, you don't see it as often as I would expect, considering the quality and ownership.

But, good news! It now comes in a 70cl bottle for around £35. Yes, you might wince a little at the price but you'll thank me when you get it in a glass.

PALMERS 44

Distillery:	The Langley Distillery, Langley Green, Warley, West Midlands
Website:	www.palmersgin.com
Visitor Centre:	No
Strength:	44%

This gin thing – it's all very new, right? Well, wrong, actually. Gin has been around and causing trouble for several centuries, but it is true that lots of the people making it and the brands they offer us are very new indeed. However, and it's an important however, even a new gin can have an old story.

Unless you've been reading this book carefully, you probably won't have heard of W. H. Palmer, the Langley Distillery or their operating business Alcohols Ltd. But they make a number of the gins listed here and a great many more. If you have an idea for a new gin (cannabis-infused, perhaps – no, too late, that one's taken), you take your concept and your chequebook to them, and they will help you realise the dream. Then you have to package, sell and market it, which is when you realise it was really a nightmare.

In its quiet and largely anonymous way, the Langley Distillery has been serving the drinks industry since 1902 and Palmers themselves go back nearly a century prior to that. Over the years, they've collected quite an array of different shapes and sizes of stills, including the McKay which reputedly dates back to the mid-1800s. It's a curious fact that gin stills virtually never wear out – just their distillers.

However, for their first eponymous venture into marketing, Palmers have elected to employ Angela, the family's copper pot which was built in 1903. Palmers 44 is, as you might expect, distilled following traditional gin distillation methods. The botanicals – juniper, coriander, angelica, cassia, liquorice, orris and grapefruit – are steeped overnight in 100% English wheat spirit while being warmed, allowing the botanicals to release their essential oils. It's a classic London Dry, shorn of any gimmicks, and can't fail to please the more traditional end of the market (like me).

But it does raise an interesting question, as Palmers claim to be responsible for distilling over 300 stock gin recipes as well as creating bespoke recipes for over 80% of the UK's artisanal brands. Can they serve two masters? Contract distilling is all very well, but trouble may lie ahead when you start to compete with your own customers. It will be interesting to see how this long-established firm of specialists will fare as they move outside their known area of expertise.

Whatever the outcome, though, this is a promising start. Shame it's taken them over 200 years to get around to it!

PISTON

Distillery:	Piston Distillery, Royal Porcelain Works, Severn Street, Worcester
Website:	www.pistongin.com
Visitor Centre:	Shop and gin school
Strength:	42%

The famous Royal Worcester porcelain factory closed in September 2006, after more than 250 years in operation, leaving a gap in the life of this lovely city. The site then lay empty but has recently been redeveloped to include a museum of fine and rare Royal Worcester ware, a café and delicatessen, an intimate theatre/concert space, some very smart luxury townhouses and, best of all, this small distillery. It's a great example of positive urban regeneration, close to the centre of the city and just off the walkway along the bank of the Severn. On the nearby 1378 Water Gate, if you look closely, you may just make out the carved outline of a giant sturgeon, so, as well as gin, there's much to see and enjoy in Worcester.

Enough tourist brochure stuff – let's get the obvious joke out of the way. 'Piston Gin' isn't what it might sound like to coarser ears but a reference to the petrolhead enthusiasm of owner Nick Weatherall, whose appreciation of engineering detail shows through in the sculpted industrial-looking bottle and stainless-steel cap, which is almost a work of art in its own right.

I was able to visit the distillery shortly after it opened and spent some time with Nick discussing his plans. I came away struck by his drive and determination to succeed and wrote shortly afterwards that I was 'really impressed. This piston fires on all cylinders – a very impressive debut from an exciting new distillery.'

My high hopes for their development have been fully justified. Today, Piston offers an innovative and unusual range of gins. Starting with their Distinguished London Dry, this includes Ginger, Forêt Noire, Oak Aged, Strawberry and Hibiscus, Douglas Fir and Coffee Infused. This latter expression blends cold-brewed Ethiopian coffee and dark Muscovado sugar with Piston gin – perfect for an Espresso Martini. They've even done something rather unusual involving the infusion of genuine ash wood from the Morgan Motor Company in nearby Malvern.

All are available in standard 70cl bottles as well as convenient and rather good-looking 20cl minis, which are ideal for trying a new style before committing to a full bottle. They are far too handsome to end up in the recycling.

The distillery itself is well equipped but compact. No visitor centre as such but a small shop and popular evening gin schools are available for a hands-on experience.

POLLINATION

Distillery:	Dyfi Distillery, Upper Corris, Machynlleth, Wales
Website:	www.dyfidistillery.com
Visitor Centre:	Yes
Strength:	45%

How green was my valley. Well, very in the case of the Dyfi Valley on the edge of the Snowdonia National Park. So green in fact that UNESCO have designated it a 'World Biosphere Reserve'.

And in this special yet fragile place, brothers Pete and Danny Cameron make their Dovey Native Botanical Gin with locally foraged rowanberries, rosehips, sloes, hawthorn, elderflower, bog myrtle, bramble and birch leaves, meadowsweet, cicely, heather and lemon balm. There's juniper in there as well, along with lemon rind, liquorice and almonds from beyond the valley which combine with another baker's dozen of botanicals, pure spring water and British wheat spirit to make up Pollination – winner of the 2017 Great British Food Awards 'Best UK Gin', collected the following year for their Dyfi Original.

Having farmed, foraged and kept bees in Dyfi for more than thirty years, Pete knows this land well. Brother Danny adds drinks business expertise, enabling him to source white port casks in which to age their Hibernation gin, one of the better cask-aged gins it's been my pleasure to try. Like Navigation, the fourth gin in the range (based around shoreline botanicals and aged in a 140-year-old vintage Madeira barrel), production is very, very limited.

That's true of everything they make, as theirs is a meticulous and demanding approach. Working with a custom-built 327-litre pot still from Müller, complete with three bubble plates, dephlegmator and offset gin basket, the need to hand-forage the botanicals is an immediate constraint. If they can't be found, there can't be any distilling, and Dyfi typically distils only once weekly. It's commercial madness, and their accountant isn't impressed.

So, as you would expect, their gins are simply but beautifully packaged. Using a distinctive tall bottle, the label wraps round to virtually join up at the back. A montage of botanicals features a loosely drawn bee (naturally enough on Pollination) and the top of the label is cut to shape to fit around the illustration. Each bottle is signed and dated by hand. They're quite gorgeous.

Pollination offers up a fresh and grassy nose with lavender and juniper notes that leads you naturally into the taste: spicy, slightly sweet and creamy, with lots of body to carry tonic or stand out in your favourite cocktail. They appreciate curious and enthusiastic gin hunters, offering the original welcome in the hillside.

PORTOBELLO ROAD

Distillery:	Thames Distillers, Timbermill Way, Clapham, London
Website:	www.portobelloroadgin.com
Visitor Centre:	Yes. The Ginstitute, 186 Portobello Road, London
Strength:	42%

With several hundred gin brands now on the market and – believe me – more arriving every week, it's genuinely hard to create something new that has the vital point of difference that will pull in drinkers. And that's if you can convince the notoriously hard-bitten trade buyers who are constantly being pitched new ideas. Which, of course, they take great relish in crushing with their renowned cynicism and world-class brutality (rather like publishers).

So, for Portobello Road to have come up with a brand that was very quickly stocked in at least one major supermarket is a considerable achievement – all the more so when, in essence, it came about accidentally. When proprietors Ged Feltham, Jake Burger and Paul Lane were experimenting with (very) small-scale distilling for their Ginstitute Museum located above their Portobello Star pub, this product took on a life of its own. And that is all the more remarkable when you consider that at that stage they were essentially pub and club operators and the museum was simply an idea to fill empty floors above the pub.

Today, having moved a few doors along the road from the Portobello Star, the Ginstitute is a splendid place to learn more about gin. Not only does the team produce craft spirits in the Ginstitute's new home, but it also houses two bars, hotel rooms and a host of experiences for visitors. Small-batch expressions such as their Navy Strength, Celebrated Butter Gin, Old Tom, Sloeberry & Blackcurrant, Savoury Gin and Temperance Low Alcohol Spirit (aaargh, the very thought of it) are produced here.

The considerably larger volume of the original London Dry style means that production had to be turned over to Charles Maxwell at Thames Distillers, who was able to scale up the quantities in his Tom Thumb still. However, it's not just the gin – excellent though it is – that stands out, as the bottle resembles a classic cognac bottle, and the label, clearly designed with a great love of Victorian graphics, combines nostalgia with contemporary shelf appeal and visual impact. Despite the arrival of a host of competitors and an increasingly crowded market, nothing else looks quite like Portobello Road, and that is a very hard trick to pull off, especially when started by accident, not design.

ROCK ROSE

Distillery:	Dunnet Bay Distillers, Dunnet, Caithness
Website:	www.dunnetbaydistillers.co.uk
Visitor Centre:	Yes
Strength:	41.5%

Here's a truly hand-crafted Scottish gin that, in just a few short weeks, achieved quite a splash of attention and made a healthy start on the goal to sell 10,000 bottles a year (that's a lot for a small start-up operation). What's more, it's in about as remote a location as you can imagine anywhere in mainland Britain and, while setting it up, co-founder Martin Murray spent around half his time on an oil rig in the North Sea where he worked as a process engineer.

That's a big part of the success. Having qualified at Heriot-Watt University, Martin and wife Claire longed to return home to Caithness and set up their own brewing and distilling business. So, Martin obtained further experience with the university's School of Brewing and Distilling and, after a lot of research and trials, was able to set up his own distillery in Dunnet Bay, in late 2014.

The still was manufactured to a unique design by John Dore & Company and features an unusual stainless-steel body with a copper dome and column; the result is efficient heating, combined with lots of copper contact in the condensing phase – so important to flavour in the spirit. All the botanicals are contained in a separate Carterhead-style basket to preserve the delicacy of the locally sourced ingredients. They, too, are a little unusual: as well as the regulation juniper and the more conventional cardamom, Martin and Claire are using rose root, sea buckthorn, rowan (keeps away the witches, as we know) and blaeberries. The result of these, and a few secret others, together with long, slow distillation and vapour infusion, is a light, fragrant and floral gin with a most attractive and distinctive nose that doesn't lack for body or mouthfeel.

A small business such as this has an inbuilt advantage at the capital investment stage as it can qualify for substantial grants from Scotland's enterprise agencies (as this did). But it still requires great personal commitment of time and money (well over £100,000 in this case) and the challenges of the remote location never go away.

If you ever tackle the North Coast 500 road trip, take the time to visit the distillery: their Rock Rose, Pink Grapefruit and Sloe gins are very fine products indeed. They speak volumes about what can be achieved with talent, energy and some lovely local botanicals. But bring a designated driver!

ROKU

Distillery:	Suntory Liquor Atelier Distillery, Minato-ku, Osaka, Japan
Website:	www.rokugin.suntory.com/en/gb
Visitor Centre:	Yes
Strength:	43% (47% in Japan)

Y ou wait for ages and three come along at once. Buses in the rain? No, Japanese gins. Virtually no gin having been distilled in Japan in living memory, we now have three to compare. That's gin made in Japan, because there are Japanese-inspired gins made in the UK but, as we're being a bit purist here, they don't count.

You could say that I should get out more, but the thing is they are very well made, very good and they bring some real variety to the more-or-less standard botanicals that appear more-or-less everywhere. And, even more excitement, they're really quite different from each other, with very distinct personalities.

This Roku, for example, comes from the giant Suntory group – Japan's largest distiller and now a global force in the spirits industry. It's made in the grandly named Liquor Atelier, a separate operation within the Yamazaki Distillery in Osaka, and in effect a specialised craft distillery for Suntory's more unusual spirits and liquors. Without slipping too far into cliché, it's made with a distinctly Japanese attention to detail that is close to obsessive. And all the better for it.

For example, four different types of pot still are used to distil the fourteen botanicals separately, according to the nature of each, as the distillery seeks to extract the best flavour while maintaining their individual characteristics. The delicate cherry blossom is prepared in a stainless-steel pot still (a most unusual vessel) under vacuum where other, more robust botanicals are distilled in copper.

The botanicals are carefully selected: eight traditional varieties for an authentic gin taste and six Japanese botanicals cultivated over four seasons and harvested at their peak to add a distinctive twist to the final blend. The search for perfection continues into the packaging, which is a thing of beauty. Naturally, the bottle features six facets to reflect the six botanicals (roku is Japanese for 'six'), and the label design and even the paper have been selected to further highlight Japanese craftsmanship and sentiment. The whole ensemble works elegantly together, and is harmonious and graceful.

Naturally, there is a recommended serve and even a special Roku measuring cup – it's suggested that you dispense 5cl (basically a double) directly into a pre-poured glass of ice and tonic, garnished with strips of fresh ginger. It's not what you expect, but isn't that exactly the point? Moreover, it's excellent. *Kampai!*

SACRED

Distillery:	Sacred Microdistillery, 50 Highgate, London
Website:	www.sacredgin.com
Visitor Centre:	Bottle shop and tasting room at 50 Highgate High Street, London
Strength:	40%

Imagine, if you will, gin as a work of art, something that you might find on the wall of the Tate. No need – it exists, because these guys make it for them. But this is an exhibit that you get to consume – making you, you might say, part of the artwork itself. Or perhaps making it a conceptual artwork. Next stop, the Turner Prize.

One of the very first microdistilling operations, Sacred now makes around 1,000 bottles a week – not bad for a distillery that started in a room in a private house in North London. That must have been an interesting conversation with the neighbours.

Joint owner and distiller Ian Hart is a refugee from the City, who turned to distilling when the financial world broke bad. Fewer bankers and more distillers: that would be my solution to greater Gross National Happiness (GNH).

Actually, Sacred does in many ways exemplify the GNH approach to life. Everything is produced by hand in their own unique design of low-pressure cold-vacuum distilling apparatus. Nothing is rushed: the twelve botanicals at the heart of Sacred's gins are all macerated for up to a month and a half before being distilled separately then blended to individual recipes and bottled at 40%.

Not so very long ago, the idea of cold distilling under a vacuum seemed eccentric and doomed to failure. But the quality of Sacred's products soon convinced bartenders that here was something special, and other brands have followed. So, I salute the ingenious Mr Hart as the first to use vacuum distillation to create gin which, by the way, uses less than 10% of the energy required by a traditional still. Everything is designed to his specification and subject to constant evolution. If it suddenly occurs to him how a particular piece of equipment might be improved, he adjusts the design accordingly.

Apart from the sustainability and the reduced capital cost, the huge benefit of cold distillation is that it maintains the freshness and vibrancy of the more delicate botanicals, something of a signature note in Sacred's products. With his meticulous small-batch approach and insistence on hands-on production, Ian Hart is not going to conquer the world of gin but he has the satisfaction of having changed it.

Sacred make masses of other interesting things: English Vermouth, whisky, vodka, Rosehip Cup and so on – all landmark products that everyone interested in interesting drinks should try.

SAFFRON

Distillery:	Maison Gabriel Boudier, 14 Ruede Cluj, Dijon, France
Website:	www.boudier.com
Visitor Centre:	No
Strength:	40%

You probably know Gabriel Boudier for their Crème de Cassis de Dijon – a product so highly esteemed they were awarded the Légion d'honneur, France's highest decoration. Think of it as the nearest thing to a republican Royal Warrant and you'll get the idea.

They have been making their liqueurs since 1874 so they know a thing or two about distilling. The company is still family-owned and distinctively French in style – something expressed wonderfully well in their ornate labels. Saffron's label is quite restrained by their standards but, delightfully, is actually printed on tin, not paper, an idiosyncratic touch that I greatly appreciated. But that, of course, is not what you first notice about this gin …

Yes, it's the colour – perhaps uncomfortably close to a glass of Irn-Bru, not that that distinctive beverage is frequently quaffed in Dijon, or indeed in the sophisticated cocktail bars that are the natural habitat of this product. The colour is derived from saffron, reputedly the most expensive of spices and one that was apparently used in the nineteenth century in a recipe discovered in the Boudier archive. Though think of India during this period as a British colony, there were French outposts in Pondicherry, Chandernagor and Madras, and Indian spices were imported to Europe where they found their way into gin.

Whether because of cost – or because it doesn't seem, to me at least, to sit well in gin – saffron never really established a place as a key botanical and isn't much used today. Diplôme, Cadenhead's Old Raj Gin and English Saffron, with their pale straw colour, are the only other ones that come to mind. Other than that, the botanicals in Boudier's version are fairly conventional: juniper, coriander, lemon, orange peel, angelica seeds, iris and fennel all feature. The saffron is added after distillation, making this a distilled gin probably best enjoyed in a cocktail (a Negroni, with its orange twist, works rather well).

Saffron Gin, despite its distinguished producer, is something of an outlier. Its colour marks it out from other gins and will offend the purist. It doesn't feel that well balanced to me, and the saffron tends to dominate and mask the other flavours. However, it's certainly one to try, although probably more as an occasional novelty rather than as part of your established drinking repertoire.

SHARISH BLUE MAGIC

Distillery:	Sharish Distillery, Reguengos de Monsaraz, Portugal
Website:	www.sharishgin.pt
Visitor Centre:	Yes
Strength:	40%

Talk about an overnight success. Only a few years ago, António Cuco was an unemployed tourism teacher, occasionally helping out at his parents' restaurant. He fancied distilling his own gin, so he cut a hole in an old pressure cooker for a still and linked it via some coiled copper piping to an empty 10-litre plastic container that had previously held olive oil – as you might do if you aren't unduly concerned about blowing yourself up or a visit from a member of the Portuguese constabulary.

By 2014, he had acquired a qualification in distilling and, perhaps more importantly, two 300-litre stills lovingly nicknamed the Minions (makes a change from women's names). Sharish Original was followed by the sensation that is Blue Magic – a deep blue gin that changes colour when tonic is added. It's a science thing: apparently the extract of flowers from the blue pea (Clitoria ternatea) reacts to the citric acid in tonic, causing the colour to flush purple or pink, depending how much tonic you put in.

It's an extremely dramatic and unexpected effect that adds to the theatre of serving a G&T in the giant goblets so beloved of bars in the Iberian peninsula. Unfortunately, we didn't get off to the best of starts with this, Mrs B. observing that the gin itself 'looks like methylated spirits' (which she doesn't drink). However, I thought it was great fun, and the market seems to agree – Sharish have gone from strength to strength, first in Portugal and then in export markets. A few imitators have piled in, and even good old Marks & Spencer now offer a colour-changing gin.

However, this was, I think, the first with the effect, and the presentation also stands out on a shelf, being reminiscent of a bottle of Mateus Rosé and with a distinctive cut-out label featuring a profile of the medieval Templar castle of Monsaraz. Be aware, though, that it's a 50cl bottle which pushes the standard UK bottle retail price equivalent dangerously close to £50.

Original is, as the name suggests, the first Sharish gin; Laurinius is cask-aged for a year to add a gentle depth and richness to the flavour; and Pera Rocha is a limited-edition style using a pear variety native to Portugal. And there's also a new Centro Interpretativo do Gin at the distillery.

SHINING CLIFF

Distillery: White Peak Distillery, Derwent Wire Works, Matlock Road, Ambergate, Derbyshire

Website: www.whitepeakdistillery.co.uk

Visitor Centre: Yes

Strength: 45%

Like many new start-ups, White Peak aim to distil whisky in due course. Yes, English whisky in the Peak District – it's a thing. Do try to keep up!

But, for the moment, they've joined in the gin boom and offer some intriguing and rather different products. The lead is their Floral Gin but they also offer Citrus, Spiced and Bakewell Pud varieties. That last was a new one to me, but involves toasted almonds, vanilla and cherries amongst the botanicals and then a final stage in which the spirit is soaked in more cherries for greater fruitiness. Well, they are just down the road from Bakewell and as almost anything seems to go in flavoured gins these days, why not?

The distillery, quite impressive in scale and ambition for a business that started as recently as 2016, is housed in an old wire works amidst the woodlands of a World Heritage site, and the naming and packaging of their various expressions is frequently inspired by local lore. There are attractively priced half-sized bottles available to encourage trial purchases, suggesting a shrewd business brain behind this operation.

A young but experienced distilling team has come on board (as well as the whisky, they're also experimenting with a Derbyshire Rum, which sounds interesting). There's a commendable commitment to local community initiatives, and this sense of place is reflected in every aspect of the business.

Though Shining Cliff's Bakewell Pud flavour might suggest a somewhat frivolous approach – and gin traditionalists will look askance at this and the other unorthodox-flavoured gins that are on the market today – I see it as combining a sense of fun with experimentation and innovation, rooted in the distillery's Derbyshire home. We can take too serious and purist an attitude to life and gin. Gin should be fun, at least in my book. Flavoured gins won't take over the world and no one is twisting your arm to buy them.

In any event, the other gins are relatively restrained twists on the classic London Dry style, with the key flavour note clearly indicated by the name. Hence Floral leads with rosehip, bilberry and local mayflower, and Citrus, probably my favourite, offers notes derived from citrus peel, lemon thyme, lime tree leaves and lemon verbena, all the while keeping the faith with a firm juniper backbone.

SHORTCROSS

Distillery:	Rademon Estate Distillery, Downpatrick, County Down, Northern Ireland
Website:	www.shortcrossgin.com
Visitor Centre:	Yes
Strength:	46%

First impressions really count, and Shortcross have done exceptionally well here. Despite using a fairly bland standard bottle, the label is outstanding. The use of letterpress printing (I'm always a sucker for a nice piece of letterpress printing), the carefully selected typefaces and subtle use of foiling on the label, not to mention the clever way the batch number is hidden on the reverse, means you can happily spend some time exploring the label before even thinking of opening the bottle. That may sound as if I need to get out more, but there's no denying the appeal of a satisfyingly tactile and well-designed piece of packaging. I was half sold on Shortcross before I even tasted it, as everything about the presentation told me that this gin had been made by people who cared, and naturally I expected that to be reflected in a quality product.

That's where the problem started. Shortcross have chosen to seal the bottle with a heavy black wax: it looks great, but took me as long to get off as I had spent savouring the label. These wax seals are the very devil to remove. You end up hacking at them with a knife, placing your fingers in considerable peril of being sliced off, and generally end up with little bits of wax all over the place.

But it was worth it in the end. Owners Fiona and David Boyd-Armstrong have gone to considerable pains to create something rather special for what is Northern Ireland's first boutique gin, and they've set the bar high. Apart from the lovely label (did I mention that?), the care and long planning is apparent in their choice of equipment.

Quite a number of small distillers use stills from Carl of Germany. Few have gone for a 450-litre copper pot still linked to two enrichment columns, each with seven individual bubble plates. It's a fine-looking piece of equipment that permits close control of the reflux during distillation, contributing to the delivery of a very smooth yet characterful spirit. With this particular design's flexibility, Shortcross have expanded their range to offer new styles including Citrus Drizzle, Cask Aged Gin and a Bartender Series.

The Boyd-Armstrongs wanted to create a gin with local provenance, hence foraged wild clover and homegrown green apples. There are elderflowers and elderberries in the botanicals: the result is sweet but not cloying, with a satisfyingly spicy and herbal finish.

SILENT POOL

Distillery:	Silent Pool Distillery, Shore Road, Albury, Surrey
Website:	www.silentpooldistillers.com
Visitor Centre:	Yes
Strength:	43%

By contrast with the youthful team one has come to expect at a craft distillery, Silent Pool can field a team of grizzled veterans. It includes three highly qualified distillers (led by Master Distiller Tom Hutchings, a noted graduate of the renowned Heriot-Watt University distilling course), a commercially experienced veteran of the UK drinks distribution scene and a couple of seasoned business executives who remain discreetly in the shadows.

And despite being one of the newer operations mentioned here, it's clear that they know exactly what they are doing. An impressive Arnold Holstein copper pot still with a seven-plate rectifying column and 'gin head' has been commissioned, allowing huge variation in creating different spirits (plans include whisky, vodka and liqueurs). Interestingly, the still itself is powered by steam from a wood-fired boiler.

The location, in a renovated barn on the Duke of Northumberland's Albury Estate, is most attractive. The name comes from a local beauty spot, the Silent Pool, part of the Surrey Hills Area of Outstanding Natural Beauty. The pool itself, from which the distillery will draw water, is said to be sacred, linked to the thirteenth-century legend of a beautiful young woodcutter's daughter who bathed in the pure, clear waters. One day, a nobleman rode by and, overcome by her beauty, approached her (the beast!). But rather than submit to his advances, she waded deeper into the water and drowned. Her father recognised the man as King John, and to this day locals claim that the girl can still be spotted at the Silent Pool at midnight.

Well, I'm convinced, and you won't catch me there at midnight, beautiful girl or not.

Along with Cory Mason, an American who has worked in top bars and craft distilling in the USA for more than fifteen years, Tom Hutchings helped create the unique four-stage distillation method for Silent Pool and sourced a number of interesting botanicals, including locally grown kaffir limes, pear and honey. His work led to his International Spirits Challenge Rising Star Award of 2020.

With their strong industry credentials and attractive packaging, I expected in my earlier book on gin that Silent Pool would achieve rapid distribution in the best cocktail bars. My confidence was well placed – they have made quite a splash and, unlike the legendary local lovely, seem to be swimming strongly to an island of profit.

SIPSMITH

Distillery:	Sipsmith Distillery, 83 Cranbrook Road, Chiswick, London
Website:	www.sipsmith.com
Visitor Centre:	Yes
Strength:	41.6%

First there was Bombay, then Hendrick's, but if any one single brand can be said to have kick-started boutique craft gin distillation in the UK it is Sipsmith. Not, of course, that they intended to do that, but the purposefully wacky guys wrote the book on small-batch, hand-crafted, artisanal, authentic – all the adjectives, in fact, beloved of the latest generation of distillers.

Their story begins in January 2007 when two old friends, Fairfax Hall and Sam Galsworthy, quit their jobs, sold their respective houses and determined to actually create the distillery they'd been talking about. By a remarkable set of happy coincidences, they found a suitable property (formerly the late great Michael Jackson's tasting room) that had once been a microbrewery. Two years of 'discussion' with HM Revenue & Customs to obtain a distilling licence then followed – for which perseverance, every subsequent small distiller should give daily thanks.

Drinks writer Jared Brown joined them as distiller and mastered the fine intricacies of Prudence, their original Christian Carl still. The bespoke design, combining a pot with a Carterhead and a column, makes for incredible versatility, allowing distillation of both vodka and gin from one apparatus. Production began in March 2009 and initial deliveries were made by hand, using Galsworthy's moped! Order after order followed, as gin took hold of the imagination of London's mixologists and their customers; less than a year later, major supermarkets and off-licences were stocking the brand, and very soon after that, a second still, Patience, was installed.

Several other expressions, including the mighty VJOP, have followed; and then came a move to enlarged premises in Chiswick with further distillation capacity in the form of Constance, their third still. Then, of course, the big boys came calling, and in December 2016, Sipsmith was bought by Beam Suntory. The partners, still all active in the business, are rightly proud of what has been achieved and are now focusing on B-Corp certification, innovative 'closed loop' recycling initiatives with a major supermarket, zero landfill and eventual carbon neutrality.

Sipsmith has achieved incredible growth in a very short time and is something of a poster boy for the craft-distilling movement. While inspiring many others to follow in Sipsmith's footsteps, few will quite as successful, or as well rewarded, but if they have half the fun and make gin half as good, their ventures will be exciting ones.

ST. GEORGE TERROIR

Distillery:	St. George Spirits, 2601 Monarch Street, Alameda, California, USA
Website:	www.stgeorgespirits.com
Visitor Centre:	Distillery tours available
Strength:	45%

Wow! Just, wow! The first time I tasted this, it absolutely took my breath away, such is the unexpected nature of the taste and the explosive impact of the first sip. And it was just as remarkable on the second and subsequent occasions. In fact, I think I can say that, of all the gins I've tasted in quite some time, this is the one that lingered longest and I could recall most distinctly the next day.

Of course, that's not always a good thing. I can think of one or two that were memorable for all the wrong reasons – they didn't make the cut, needless to say – but, while this is a love-it-or-hate-it kind of a spirit, it's clearly made with a point of view. Or perhaps attitude would be more apt, for this hails from St. George Spirits in Alameda, California, arguably the birthplace of the modern American artisan distillation movement. This distillery was founded in 1982 by Jörg Rupf, a German immigrant with family connections to the distilling of fruit spirits in the Black Forest, who wanted to recreate the products he remembered from Germany. In the process, he changed everything that was then known about distilling in the USA.

Several other very well-known artisan distillers in the USA trained here and have gone on to establish their own operations, often with considerable success. And St. George's, now owned by Lance Winters, has grown to the point where it now occupies a 65,000-square-foot building and operates a number of stills, making a full range of spirits.

They describe Terroir as 'a profoundly aromatic gin with a real sense of place', suggesting that 'Terroir is a forest in your glass'. Included in the botanicals are Douglas fir, California bay laurel and coastal sage along with roasted coriander seeds and nine other more conventional botanicals. They distil the fir and sage individually in a 250-litre still to minimise the impact of seasonal variation, while the fresh bay laurel leaves and juniper berries are vapour-infused in a botanicals basket and the other botanicals go right into their 1,500-litre pot still. The result is a walk in the pinewoods.

It's remarkable. I suspect some recent converts to gin would find it challenging but I went back to the glass time after time, if only to confirm that I hadn't imagined its dramatic, intense aromas and taste.

I'm pining for it now.

STRANE
MERCHANT
STRENGTH

Distillery:	Smögen Whisky AB, Hunnebostrand, Sweden
Website:	www.strane.se
Visitor Centre:	Distillery tours available by appointment
Strength:	47.4%

STRANE

London Dry Gin
MERCHANT STRENGTH

COPPER POT DISTILLED OVER A LIVE FLAME
CHOICE CHARACTER FROM SUPREME BOTANICALS

| 500 MILLILITERS | 47.4 % ALCOHOL BY VOLUME | MASTER BLEND |

G in? From a whisky distillery? In Sweden? Yes, it's all true. Smögen Whisky was established in 2010 by lawyer and whisky author turned distiller Pär Caldenby and has proved one of the success stories of Swedish craft distilling (there have been failures).

They make three gins, all in small quantities, in a tiny 100-litre gas-fired direct-flame pot still. True to their whisky roots, blending is at the heart of what they do, and the production process at Strane is both interesting and unusual. Actually, Hendrick's does something similar and, curious but true, that's also made by a company better known for its whisky.

Beginning with the same twelve botanicals (juniper, coriander, sage, lime and lemon peel, basil, mint, sweet almond, cinnamon, liquorice and two secret ingredients native to Sweden), Caldenby uses them to create three separate distillates with distinct flavours. The separate distillates – not finished gins at this stage – one junipery, the second citrus-dominated and the third more herbal are then blended in different ratios to create three final products. Simples! Whisky blenders do this all the time, except they use the products of different distilleries and varying cask types.

The thinking behind this is to emphasise and consistently deliver the flavour of each group of botanicals, exploiting the fact that different botanicals behave differently at different boiling points. Rather than adopting a 'one size fits all' approach, this allows the team scope to explore the subtler notes in each.

The base spirits are then blended to produce the three expressions, Merchant, Navy and Uncut – all are bottled at different strengths and quite distinctive in style and flavour. Of course, the key to product consistency then lies in the blending, exactly like a blended Scotch whisky. The first and most widely available is their Merchant Strength, a chunky 47.4% bruiser; the Uncut reaches an alarming 76% abv. Sadly, it's been discontinued though some remains available at time of writing.

Gin made like this, at a higher strength, in small batches, from a high-wage economy such as Sweden's, is never going to be cheap. You'll find Strane in a few UK specialists at around £40 for their 50cl bottle (the equivalent of £56 for a standard bottle), which pushes it into super-premium territory. So, it's probably more of a special treat than an everyday tipple, unless those secret Swedish botanicals really float your boat.

TANQUERAY
No. 10

Distillery:	Diageo Cameronbridge Distillery, Leven, Fife
Website:	www.tanqueray.com
Visitor Centre:	No
Strength:	47.3%

Here's proof – if proof were needed – that big brands can be cool, sexy and very, very good. Because this super-premium expression of one of the USA's favourite gins is all those things. It's what's in the bottle that counts, and here we have a gin that any distiller would be proud to offer up, any fashionable cocktail watering hole happy to mix, and any discerning drinker more than content to savour.

Tanqueray started life in London in 1830 but has had an itinerant existence since the Second World War. It's now settled in its own dedicated gin hall located within Diageo's giant Cameronbridge distilling complex – unfortunately, so large and so busy that public access will never be possible. Never mind, I popped in to take a look and I can report it is both hugely impressive and reassuringly calm. The venerable Old Tom No. 4a still and its diminutive fellow Tiny Tim both seem well settled in their Scottish home. Both are vital to Tanqueray Ten; the citrus heart of the spirit is first distilled in Tiny Tim using fresh chopped oranges, limes and grapefruit, and this is then transferred to the larger, hand-riveted Old Tom, where juniper (more than in the standard version), coriander, angelica, liquorice, camomile flowers and more limes are added.

In order to preserve the vibrant citrus character, only 60% of the final run is selected to go forward for reduction and eventual bottling. Unusually, Tanqueray is made using the one-shot process – another nod to tradition and further evidence of the carefully crafted nature of this superb creation. Finally, I'm glad to say that it's reassuringly strong (something to remember when comparing prices). At 47.3% this offers body, mouthfeel and a delightfully mouth-coating creaminess. It is a stone-cold classic that continues to deliver from aroma to finish and is great in cocktails.

Indeed, I'd go so far as to say that you might never need to try another gin ever again. But, having experimented with Rangpur (lime) and Flor de Sevilla (oranges), Tanqueray have clearly decided to embrace flavours. These were limited editions but received so positively that they're now permanent members of the family and, most recently, have been joined by Blackcurrant Royale (you can probably guess this one), but, if baffled, you'll find more details in the Pink Gins chapter.

I don't usually do marks, but it's so very good and such great value that I have to give Ten 10/10!

TARQUIN'S

Distillery:	Southwestern Distillery, Higher Trevibban Farm, St Ervan, Wadebridge, Cornwall
Website:	www.tarquinsgin.com
Visitor Centre:	Yes
Strength:	42%

This makes quite the contrast with the previous entry, Tanqueray. Here we are with Tarquin Leadbetter of the eponymous Tarquin's gin, which one could describe as bold, experimental, innovative and quite funky. All the things a small craft distiller is supposed to be, though Tarquin's isn't that small any more. In fact, on my last trip to Cornwall, it was everywhere, and they now claim to be the twenty-ninth fastest-growing company and the second biggest independent distillery within the UK. That sounds ominously like an invitation …

From a standing start in July 2013, using a second-hand still bought for €200 off eBay and heated by a large gas ring, the distillery has expanded to the point where they can be producing close to 5,000 bottles a day in busy periods. As you may imagine, distilling is a rather more sophisticated operation these days, with larger stills, though here they still hand-bottle, -pour, -wax and -pack every single bottle. There are shops in St Ives and Padstow, and the original distillery space on the farm is now a popular visitor centre.

Starting out, Tarquin picked some unusual but not completely outrageous botanicals, including fresh citrus fruits, cacao, pink peppercorns and violet leaves but has gone on to develop some thirty special editions of small-batch releases, ranging from Cornish seaweed to Earl Grey tea. At the heart of this experimentation is his early training and experience as a chef, backed up by the business acumen and drive of his sister Athene. While success came quickly, it was preceded by countless experiments and the trial and error of a self-taught distiller confident in his own taste and judgement – though it was finally the drudgery of a life in City banking that drove him home to Cornwall (I'm not quite clear how a trained chef ends up in finance but that's another chapter in their story).

Today, the core range comprises Cornish Dry, Seadog Navy, British Blackberry, Blood Orange, Rhubarb & Raspberry and Elderflower & Pink Grapefruit. Just to add to the fun, in the middle of 2020, pandemic or not, they launched their Twin Fin Rum.

I've not mentioned the awards, but, take it from me, they have quite a large trophy cabinet. Good luck to them: anyone who can distil the UK's first aniseed spirit and call it Cornish Pastis deserves to succeed!

THREE RIVERS

Distillery:	City of Manchester Distillery, 21 Red Bank Parade, Manchester
Website:	www.manchesterthreerivers.com
Visitor Centre:	Yes
Strength:	40%

What does it tell us about Manchester, or indeed gin, that in all of this fine city the number one rated Thing to Do in Manchester on TripAdvisor for over three years is the £95 Gin Experience at the City of Manchester distillery? Maybe it's because the Rum Experience is £120 – or perhaps not everyone likes football?

Remarkably, 99% of the reviewers (almost 600 of them as we go to press) rated it 'excellent' or 'very good'. So, let's conclude from the wisdom of crowds that the City of Manchester is getting something very right indeed.

It's certainly a professional outfit, with a well-organised website and some serious investment evident in the smart bar and visitor facilities, the shiny Arnold Holstein still and an impressive line-up of mini stills where visitors can make their own bottle of gin after choosing from the fifty-odd botanicals on offer. They're not alone in offering this type of interactive experience which, as well as providing a very useful revenue stream, sends a flood of eager, unpaid brand ambassadors out to spread the word. It's very good marketing and a jolly good time appears to be had by all.

There's nothing outrageous or deliberately provocative about the product itself. Not to damn with faint praise, but this is fairly mainstream, although the addition of oats enlivens an otherwise conventional mix of botanicals. Cardamom and black pepper make their presence felt alongside the regulation juniper, and it's smooth, creamy and warming. A suggested serve features a garnish of fresh cherries which is unusual but brings some pleasantly fruity notes to the fore.

The presence of those intriguing oats is a nod to the history of the nearby Angel Meadow. Apparently, the area was anything but angelic, and the impoverished inhabitants got by on meagre rations. Dr Johnson famously defined oats as 'a grain which in England is generally given to horses, but in Scotland supports the people'. (To which Boswell replied, 'Aye, and that's why England has such fine horses, and Scotland such fine people.') That was in 1755; evidently little had improved by the Victorian age for the masses more or less enslaved in the factories of the Industrial Revolution. They famously took some solace in gin. Well, things have clearly moved on and for the better.

The 'three rivers', in case you were wondering, are the Irwell, Irk and Medlock.

UNGAVA

Distillery:	291 Rue Miner, Cowansville, Quebec, Canada
Website:	www.ungavagin.com
Visitor Centre:	No
Strength:	43.1%

We haven't had a gin from Canada yet, so this piqued my curiosity. The name and packaging are funky and the colour draws the eye. Ah yes, that colour. When the company's president told Canada's *Maclean's* magazine that it was 'a bit like morning's vitamin-enriched urine', there's not a lot more to say. Mind you, it didn't put off Pernod Ricard, who bought the brand and company in August 2016 (around the same time as a small social media storm accused Ungava of cultural appropriation).

Ungava contains some seriously obscure botanicals – creating a gin that is truly, pre-colonially Canadian. So, some forty indigenous herbs, berries and flowers (anything planted by Europeans was out) gave way to six ingredients, all found on the Ungava Peninsula in Nunavik. Cloudberries, crowberries, Labrador tea, Ukiurtatuq or 'Arctic blend' (a plant used by the Inuit to make tea) and juniper, without which, of course, Ungava wouldn't be proper gin. And the crazy colour? Don't worry. That comes from the sixth ingredient, wild rosehips.

The company get pretty lyrical about Ungava (Inuit for 'towards the open water'), a vast, wild territory at the northern edge of Quebec: 'Adorned by a brilliant mantle of ice and snow for nearly nine months of the year, Ungava Bay is a place of indescribable beauty; rich in mineral wealth … an unspoiled region of startling landscapes and extreme climate.' Not so indescribable after all, but, as I haven't been there, let's take their word for it.

Once a year, two hardy Inuit chaps from Kuujjuaq head out to pick the botanicals. They've got just four weeks to harvest several hundred kilos, which are then sent about 900 miles south to a microdistillery in Cowansville, about an hour's drive from Montreal. A neutral spirit made with locally grown corn is infused with the botanicals. From start to finish, it takes more than a month to make a batch of gin, which comes out of the distillery at 72% alcohol and then gets diluted to 43.1% for bottling. Nunavik botanicals are added at the beginning of the process, and again towards the end.

The squiggles on the label aren't some meaningless jumble of lines, but Inuktitut. Sadly, I don't suppose the 'on-trend socials' who are the brand's desired consumer have the slightest idea what it means, any more than I do. But they look lovely.

VILLA ASCENTI

Distillery:	Distilleria Santa Vittoria, Villa Ascenti, Santa Vittoria, Italy
Website:	www.wearebulletproof.com/work/villa-ascenti/
Visitor Centre:	No
Strength:	40%

This luxury Italian gin, available in a conventional dry style or as the pink-flushed Rosa, is part of the Diageo stable (alongside Gordon's, Tanqueray, Jinzu and Chase) but hails from the Distilleria Santa Vittoria in Piedmont, under the watchful eye of Master Distiller Lorenzo Rosso.

With a relatively modest £360,000 budget, a distillery has been built on the site of the brand home, Villa Ascenti, which features a refurbished Frilli copper pot still from the 1970s. Relatively unfamiliar in the UK, Frilli have been renowned still makers in Tuscany for over one hundred years. Today, their stills may be seen in a couple of locations in Scotland, where they are used to make both excellent whisky and gin.

You might not immediately associate Italy with gin, though we do owe it the Negroni and, indeed, its lesser-known counterpart, the Cardinal (substitute dry vermouth for sweet and alter the proportions to favour the gin part). Maestro Rosso – I think we may extend him the courtesy of that honorific – aimed to work with local producers and farmers in the local community to source the ingredients for Villa Ascenti gin, which include Moscato grapes, fresh mint and thyme. Great stress is placed on freshness in the distillate, with the herbs reaching the still within hours of harvesting.

Moscato grapes, a signature taste of the region, are harvested in August and September when the fruit is at its best, before undergoing three distillations. During the final distillation, the Moscato grapes are infused with Tuscan juniper berries. However, despite any concern that the grapes might lend an overly sweet note, the gin itself is less sweet than might be anticipated, with the mint, thyme and juniper clearly evident. It's refreshing in a simple G&T (Fever-Tree's Mediterranean would work well) and a born natural for a Martini.

More recently, the distillery has launched a sister style, Villa Ascenti Rosa. The very subtle pink blush in the liquid comes not from berries as we might expect, but from ripe peach and Brachetto grape distillate. The peach sweetness comes to the fore, but other botanicals such as apricots, elderflower, hazelnut, achillea and Tuscan juniper berries all play their part.

If you are looking for an affordable and stylish taste of Italy, look no further.

WARNER'S HARRINGTON DRY

Distillery:	Warner's Distillery, Falls Farm, Harrington, Northamptonshire
Website:	www.warnersdistillery.com
Visitor Centre:	Yes
Strength:	44%

As I believe I may have mentioned, I hesitate to refer to anyone as 'passionate' about their product. The problem with this perfectly good, inoffensive and hitherto useful word is that it has been entirely devalued by the marketing and PR community. 'Passion' is everywhere, and as a result it's nowhere. It is a meaningless cliché that has been hollowed out and now lies dully on the page, gasping for its last breath like a stranded dolphin.

Unfortunately, I can't think of another word to describe Tom Warner's enthusiasm for his product. Talking to him, it was hard to get a word in edgeways such was the tumbling rush of ardent advocacy. Here, I felt, was a man alive with a mission to share, to explain, to proselytise about his product, so intensely felt that I may as well have been in the presence of the Ancient Mariner – not the gin of the same name but the bloke in the poem – and I could not choose but hear.

And what a great story he tells. Warners was, in December 2012, created by Tom and Tina Warner (with help from then business partner Sion Edwards, now at Union Distillers in nearby Market Harborough). Being committed to the idea of a craft gin, and wanting to do it properly, they bought one of the UK's first small Holstein stills. They've gone from strength to strength while remaining a proudly independent, family-run UK distillery.

They grow their own angelica on the family farm and use discarded orange peels from a local fruit factory that would otherwise go to waste. Great for sustainability, they provide the bright, vibrant orange flavours you just can't get using dried peels. Their concern for the environment means they're a member of 1% for the Planet and working towards B-Corp accreditation.

Since launch, the range has grown to incorporate Elderflower, Rhubarb, Raspberry, Lemon Balm, Honeybee, Sloe, 0% Botanic Garden Spirits Juniper Double Dry, 0% Pink Berry and the original London Dry.

This is a bold, juniper-led, peppery and complex product that should appeal to traditionalists willing to push the boundaries of flavour without anything too outrageous or provocatively unconventional. Use in cocktails where you really want the gin to shine through.

WHITETAIL

Distillery:	Whitetail Spirits Ltd, The Steadings, Tiroran, Isle of Mull
Website:	www.whitetailgin.com
Visitor Centre:	Café and shop.
Strength:	47%

Though we might normally associate them with single malt whisky, there is something of a gin explosion on a number of Hebridean islands, and Mull is no exception. The larger Tobermory Distillery, in the main town, has begun producing gin when not busy with whisky, but further afield, there is a smaller independent producer at Tiroran – though you won't stumble across them by accident.

Tiroran is a remote settlement on the western side of the island, sitting on the shore of Loch Scridain, where a tiny still has been installed in the steadings (a Scottish term for the outbuildings of a farm) on a family-owned estate. It's a wonderful, pristine environment, home to the White-tailed Eagle (aka the Sea Eagle). This magnificent raptor is Britain's largest bird of prey, with a huge wing span of up to 2.5 metres. Like the gin that carries its name, the White-tailed Eagle combines strength with power and a soaring grace in flight.

Fittingly, Whitetail gin is bottled at 47% and employs a range of botanicals, many locally foraged. The more usual juniper, coriander and lemon peel are present, but the real secret lies in the native Mull botanicals. These include heather, winter savory (a semi-evergreen plant, also used in herbal medicine), together with pine needles from the family estate and sea kelp collected from the lochside.

Kelp was extensively harvested during the eighteenth and nineteenth centuries and burned in special kilns to form alkali kelp ash, then used in bleaching linen and the manufacture of glass and soap. In fact, in a little over six months in 1792, more than 1,800 tons of kelp was recorded as leaving Tobermory alone. Not many people know that! However, the industry collapsed in the 1840s when synthetic methods of production took over and the seaweed's sole economic use was as fertiliser on the Hebrides' many subsistence crofts. Today, it's the source of valuable alginates, and it features in other gins including Isle of Harris and Dà Mhìle.

Alongside the gin, a small range of speciality fruit-based gin liqueurs are also produced here. In its short life, Whitetail has collected awards from the International Spirits Challenge and IWSC. Clearly, it has the potential to ruffle a few feathers.

WHITLEY NEILL

Distillery:	City of London Distillery, 22–24 Bride Lane, London
Website:	www.whitleyneill.com
Visitor Centre:	Yes
Strength:	43%

rat! More of that pesky dark glass that doesn't allow you to see how much is left in the bottle. Aren't those bottles annoying? Gin is a wonderfully clear and bright spirit, so why hide it away? (Actually one reason is that it keeps better. I just drink it faster though; that works as well.)

What we have here is another gin inspired by Africa but brought to us by Johnny Neill, a fourth-generation member of the Greenall Whitley distilling dynasty – a man with gin in his blood. He turned to the physalis plant and the baobab tree – known as the 'tree of life' – to add the flavour of Africa to this most English of spirits. The latter's otherworldly, upside-down form features as the brand's logo.

Launched in 2005, Whitley Neill was an early entrant into the small-batch gin scene and continues to collect medal after medal for its complex, spicy taste, layered earth notes, hints of tropical fruits and lemons, and peppery finish. But, in addition to medals, it seems we like it as well: independent market research suggests this is the UK's best-selling premium gin brand.

It was originally produced at the Langley Distillery in the West Midlands, but today Neill has taken gin back to its earliest English roots and the brand has found its own very special home in the City of London Distillery. There, it's produced alongside its company stablemate, a gin of the same name. The distillery, remarkably still the only one within the City boundaries, aims to maintain the heritage and history of London's gin production in the spirit's original home while looking to new contemporary ideas – see below for evidence of that. Both the Whitley Neill and City of London brands are part of the Halewood Artisanal Spirits group, who also own Aber Falls in Wales – all feature here.

The adventurous Mr Neill has embraced the idea of flavoured variants with gusto, offering a whole fruit basket of different expressions, such as – deep breath! – Raspberry, Rhubarb & Ginger, Blood Orange, Pink Grapefruit, Blackberry, Aloe & Cucumber, Parma Violet, Quince and Lemongrass & Ginger. There will undoubtedly be more by now, so check their website for the most recent offerings from their overflowing cornucopia of zesty gin goodness.

WHITTAKER'S ORIGINAL

Distillery:	Whittaker's Distillers, Harewell House Farm, Nidderdale, North Yorkshire
Website:	www.whittakersgin.com
Visitor Centre:	Yes
Strength:	42%

There are lots of awards out there for various spirits. It's something of a growth industry as shrewd publishers and various entrepreneurially minded folk note that distillers like to have little gold and silver stickers to affix to their bottles and so launch their awards to compete with the more established – and, dare I say, widely recognised – schemes. Still, one sticker looks much like another when viewed on an off-licence shelf and so the proliferation of awards continues.

Whittaker's – by now gin veterans – have been entering competitions since 2015 and have aced a good few, including awards from the IWSC and ISC, the Craft Distilling Expo and the American Distilling Institute. Now, those latter names might not mean much to you but they're indicative of Whittaker's being recognised by, and arguably rising above, their peers. Especially in the USA, where there is a very large craft-distilling scene, this represents praise indeed.

Little wonder, then, that this farm-based distillery from near Harrogate has rapidly expanded from one small 100-litre Hill Billy Stills' import from Bourbon Country in Kentucky and now employs a more substantial 500-litre still, also from the US.

The range has expanded too, to include the Original, a Navy Strength, the Summer and Winter Solstice variants and the charmingly named Pink Particular (pink peppercorns, pink hibiscus and cardamom are the signature botanicals at work here). Cleverly, they make it easy for us to try all the products, offering mini 5cl and large 70cl bottles – something that other small brands might like to copy.

Reflecting its Yorkshire antecedents, this is not a gin that's shy and bashful! Lots of earthy juniper will grab your attention, but there are hints of the lemon groves in there and drying spices to give the palate plenty to hang on to. Classy stuff.

Finally, a word on the handsome labels. With a base at Harewell House Farm, the hare was a logical and emotional choice to grace the packaging and very fine it looks, too.

WILLIAMS ELEGANT 48

Distillery:	Chase Distillery, Rosemaund Farm, Hereford
Website:	www.chasedistillery.co.uk
Visitor Centre:	Yes
Strength:	48%

Once upon a time, a hard-up Herefordshire potato farmer found there was more money in making premium crisps than selling spuds, and so Tyrrells Crisps were born. Then this entrepreneurial fellow, one William Chase, discovered small-batch potato vodka and found there was more money in making luxury spirits than premium crisps, and before long Williams Elegant 48 was born. It also used up the smaller potatoes that weren't suitable for making crisps. Handy, that.

Enter some venture capitalists who paid loadsamoney (some accounts say £40m) for the crisp company, but they soon fell out. Still, no longer hard-up, that allowed him to acquire a large yacht, a lot of property and a £3m distillery with a seventy-foot-high rectifying column (it's every bit as tall as it sounds; I went to see it, and looking up made my neck hurt). Now, I don't know about you, but I like a salty snack with my beverages. However, the venture capitalists, by now no longer the best of friends, didn't agree and so the Tyrrell name disappeared from the vodka bottles and Chase Distillery emerged – which, wouldn't you just know, he sold in October 2020 to Diageo. Who says lightning doesn't strike twice!

Chase had got in ahead of the rush to small-brand premium spirits, was well financed and smartly run by an experienced businessman, and made a fine product. Jamie Baxter, whose name you will see several times in this book, was the first distiller. Being based on a farm, Chase grows other things such as apples (this is Herefordshire, after all), and they provide the base for the vodka that they turn to gin. This isn't unique, but it is fairly unusual.

A total of 450 litres of the apple-based vodka is then placed in Ginny, a separate copper pot still with a Carterhead vapour chamber, where a pillowcase full of botanicals turns the spirit into gin prior to arriving in the small condenser. The botanicals are conventional enough, other than the addition of hops and fresh apples which seems fitting, as the distillery buildings once housed an experimental hop kiln and the National Association of Cider Makers had a trial orchard here.

The heart of the Chase success is that this is an estate-grown and estate-distilled product, which is bottled on site and thus proudly 'field to bottle'. Better still, much of the waste goes to feed their pedigree Hereford cattle. But what will the entrepreneurial Mr Chase get up to next, I wonder?

XORIGUER

Distillery:	Destilerías Xoriguer, Mahón, Menorca
Website:	www.xoriguer.co.uk
Visitor Centre:	No
Strength:	38%

Are we nearly there yet? Having begun with a numeral and then gone straight into the letter 'A', we are now nearing the end of this alphabetical romp through the wacky world of essential gins.

And thus our magic carpet transports us to the Balearic island of Menorca and Xoriguer, which turns out to have the most fascinating story imaginable. For one thing, there are only two gins left in the world that enjoy recognition as a local speciality (the other is Vilnius Gin from Lithuania). And there's a connection to the Jolly Jack Tars of Britain's Royal Navy.

In the eighteenth century, Menorca was in British hands and we had a huge naval base there. And, in the middle of the Gin Craze, what do you imagine thirsty British seafarers wanted to drink? Hint: the answer is not rum. So, the locals made gin for them and they're at it still. Today, it's mainly hot and bothered holidaymakers rather than dehydrated deckhands who patronise the island's bars in search of refreshment for their parched throats.

Unusually, rather than a neutral spirit, it is distilled using a base of Mediterranean wine alcohol and is drawn off the wood-fired stills at its 38% bottling strength. It comes in a seriously funky bottle with a label that is genuinely retro (largely because no one has got round to changing it in years). What's not to like?

It gets better. It is, of course, still family-owned and distilled to a secret recipe. Apparently, only heirs of the founder Miguel Pons Justo are permitted to receive the super-classified details and proportions of the vital ingredients, and before they add them to the still, the doors are locked and any witnesses killed. Yes, I made that last bit up – they just politely ask them to leave.

Before bottling, it is rested in oak. You can find a bottle here in the UK for under £25, which is quite the bargain, especially when the vintage bottle is included. I can't tell you how happy it has made me to track down Xoriguer (say it 'sho-ri-gair') – a truly artisanal gin, with deep and long-standing connections to the great days of English gin distilling, that is still alive and flourishing in this new Gin Craze.

ZYMURGORIUM

Distillery:	Zymurgorium, Fairhills Road, Irlam, Greater Manchester
Website:	www.zymurgorium.com
Visitor Centre:	Bar and shop
Strength:	40%

Zounds (from 'God's wounds' – an Elizabethan oath)! In the interests, if nothing else, of my zelotic (excessive zeal) alliteration, I had hoped to bring you a zesty Zebra gin distilled by some zany Zoroastrians in Zanzibar, flavoured with *zabaglione* (an Italian custard dessert) and zizyphus fruit (a spiny shrub) and served in a zegedine (a silver drinking cup) – but sadly I failed. Actually, there are a couple of Zebra gins, in Hampshire and Uganda respectively, but off we must zoom to an industrial estate in Manchester.

Zzzz! Don't drop off, for this is zoetic or full of life. [Honestly, I think that's enough z's – Ed.] You've probably never heard of a zymurgorium. Neither had I, but that's because in their zeal (sorry, it just crept in), these marvellous madcap Mancunians manufactured it in a mission to 'make every moment epic'.

A zymurgorium – they say and who are we to disagree – is a shop that sells products which have been brewed or distilled – which, not terribly coincidentally, is what they do. But I love portmanteau words, so let's see what's in their bag of tricks. Mostly some wild and wonderful gins, such as Syllabub, Mandarin Dynasty Oriental, Choc-o-Bloc, Flamingo Pink and Winter Raspberry, and, if they don't tempt you, a range of gin liqueurs including Realm of the Unicorn, Fruit Salad Pineapple & Sweet Raspberry and many, many more that you cannot begin to imagine but can try in their rather cool-looking bar.

And, most of all, respect to terrific products such as their Manchester Marmalade gin (doubtless including real zest), made in collaboration with Manchester's own Duerr's, Britain's oldest family-owned producer of preserves. For years now, UK marmalade sales have been falling. Perhaps this will convince young people to preserve this inestimable comestible. It's what Paddington would want!

Respect their energy and sense of fun. Whether Mr Gordon or Mr Tanqueray or other distilling greats from history would recognise marmalade gin is debatable. But you might term that carping and unjust criticism – or even zoilism.

Sorry, I couldn't help myself!

COASTAL
CHARMS

G in, you might argue, lies at the very heart of England. However, in actual fact, nowhere in Britain is more than seventy miles from the sea (the otherwise unremarkable hamlet of Coton in the Elms, Derbyshire is the point in Britain furthest from our shores and, predictably enough, there's a distillery less than four minutes' drive distant).* So, in truth, from the slightly-damp King Canute to today's plucky cross-Channel swimmers, from Admiral Nelson to the White Cliffs of Dover (never mind the traditional bucket-and-spade seaside holiday), we're really an island race, shaped and defined by the water that surrounds us. Or as Shakespeare would have it, we put cheerily to sea from 'this little world, This precious stone set in the silver sea'.

So, with those words ringing in my ears, it seemed fitting to explore some coastal gins. From Shetland to the Scilly Isles (about 720 miles, since you ask), all round Britain's coastline you can find a gin distillery. Indeed, at Tappers on the Wirral they even make a Coastal Gin, as do Bullards of Norwich (which is a bit of a stretch to the briny) and Badachro in the Scottish Highlands with their Gairloch Coastal Gin. And there's the Coastal Distillery at Mablethorpe, Lincolnshire between Grimsby and bracing Skegness.

The Isle of Wight Distillery brings us Mermaid Gin, while from the Three Fingers Distillery in Guernsey comes Blue Bottle Dry Gin. It has a beautiful but alarmingly detailed picture of said annoying insect on the label, so let's move along to the Poetic Licence distillery in Roker, Sunderland, who have been making their gins for more than half a decade now (that's aeons in gin-land time).

It's no mere gimmick. The more enlightened of these coastal distillers have been exploring their nearby shores to exploit locally sourced botanicals such as seaweed, samphire, sea purslane (try a few of its salty leaves in a salad or lightly steam them and serve as a vegetable) and sea buckthorn, whose small but intense berries feature in Adnam's Orange & Sea Buckthorn Gin. And you can hardly get more coastal than Southwold and the North Norfolk dunes where they forage their supplies.

*It's actually the Staffordshire Distillery where they make – go on, have a guess – lots of tasty looking gins.

Local microclimates do affect distilling in subtle and complex ways. Different varieties of seaweed, for example, grown and harvested in different locations will inevitably have their particular contributions to flavour, and the same applies to the land-based botanicals foraged from the shoreline. Salt-marsh-grown botanicals simply won't be the same as those gathered off the Hebridean *machair* – surely there's a PhD thesis waiting here for some lucky student. Just imagine the extensive sampling that would be required.

There's more, but you've got the idea. We do love to be beside the seaside, and a stiff local gin completes the pleasure. Set sail with me and read on for a few of my favourites which, for the sake of some variety, also include the Coastal Citrus gin from Sydney's Manly Spirits, representing Australia's 22,293 miles of coastline.

All together now, m'hearties!

A life on the ocean wave,
A home on the rolling deep,
Where the scattered waters rave
And the winds their revels keep!
Like an eagle caged I pine
On this dull unchanging shore,
Oh, give me the flashing brine,
The spray and the tempest's roar!

– *A Life on the Ocean Wave* (1838) by Epes Sargent

BOATYARD

Distillery:	The Boatyard Distillery, Tullybay Marina, Enniskillen, Northern Ireland
Website:	www.boatyarddistillery.com
Visitor Centre:	Yes
Strength:	40%

Here's a distillery you can reach from the water. As you've guessed from the name, it's located in an old boatyard (on the shores of Lough Erne in County Fermanagh) and is actually the county's first distillery since 1890. Well, *legal* distillery anyway, as the production of poitín isn't allegedly a complete secret in the West of Ireland to this very day. Or so I've been told.

You can't get more coastal than a boatyard on the Shore Road, though to be pedantic, it's on the shoreline of a lake. Never mind, it'll do nicely because some interesting things are made here.

Local man Joe McGirr worked in the drinks industry with Glenmorangie and with a small distillery in London before establishing Boatyard in 2016 with help from family members who still farm nearby and grow some of the botanicals, including sweet gale, which is harvested from the family's own acres. Head Distiller Órlaith Kelm is a local girl who started on the labelling team but quickly progressed to take charge of production.

There's a commendable commitment to sustainable production that's appropriate to the great natural beauty of the distillery's surroundings, with every element from bottles to business cards working towards a goal of carbon neutrality by 2023. In an unusual twist, spent botanicals even go into a gin-infused Tanzanian cocoa chocolate bar.

Production is concentrated around Double Gin and Ireland's first Old Tom, both distinctive in their own way. Double Gin refers to the fact that the spirit encounters juniper twice during the distilling process, emphasising the note of this signature botanical. The increased contact means that the gin may louche, or go slightly cloudy, when cold or diluted with tonic or another mixer. Nothing to worry about; in fact it's a reassurance that there are plenty of essential oils in the spirit delivering its pronounced flavour. A very clear graphic on the website shows the strong juniper influence. Would that all distillers offer this level of transparency and detail – not every drinker wants or needs it, but for those who do, it's fascinating.

Boatyard's Old Tom also offers much of interest to the enthusiast, being the first distiller in Ireland to offer this traditional style. But there's a great twist: their interpretation rests the gin in first-fill Pedro Ximénez casks and a small quantity of this intensely sweet sherry is also added after ageing, creating the harmonious notes of fig, candied fruits and toffee.

FISHERS

Distillery:	Fishers, Aldeburgh, Suffolk
Website:	www.fishersgin.com
Visitor Centre:	Yes
Strength:	44%

ere's a gin made in England but with its eyes originally fixed firmly across the Channel. It's one of the many new small-batch products flooding the French market as our neighbours experience their own gin boom. But now you can get it here as well, as the company has evolved to operate its own distillery in Aldeburgh. In fact, it claims to be the closest gin distillery to the coast anywhere in the UK.

It was originally distilled by Adnams, in nearby Southwold, for an entrepreneurial chap with long-standing connections to the Adnams brewing business, interests in the wine trade and strong connections to the champagne industry. However, Andrew Heald (for that is his name) always aimed to relocate to Aldeburgh, which is his birthplace, and in 2019 the distillery was commissioned.

And something else that changed was the half-litre bottle, which has been dropped in favour of the UK standard 70cl size. It's not the cheapest gin out there, but it's only fair to point out that Fisher's is being bottled at 44% rather than the more normal 40%. That means you're buying more alcohol and less water. A stronger version, Fifty, is also available at 50% and, guess what, comes in the original 50cl bottle.

On its launch in France, it was tasted there by the drinks magazine *Fine Spirits*, where it received qualified approval (you can't expect them to praise an English product *too* highly!). What did they think? One taster concluded: '*Pas du tout désagréable, juste un peu bizarre.*'

That seems a little harsh. His colleague's summary was: '*Un côté austere avec un nez rustique qui cache en fait une bouche complexe et cyclique. Intriguant!*'

Well, I imagine 'a rustic nose' and 'intriguing' were preferred to 'just a little bizarre'. I saw those reviews before first tasting the product, which is definitely not a run-of-the-mill gin. The taste is down to the addition of unusual and highly distinctive local botanicals, including spignel, wood aven, bog myrtle, rock samphire, wild angelica and wild fennel. So, yes, 'rustic' but sophisticated too.

Moving distilleries is not the simplest of tasks, as it risks some variation in flavour between batches. However, Fishers have done a fine job of capturing their coastal environment between the sea and the salt marshes. Incidentally, the scallop shell on the label was inspired by Maggi Hambling's justly celebrated sculpture, something of an icon for this very special place.

GIN OF PARADISE

Distillery:	Madame Jennifer Distillery Ltd, Poets Corner, Hove
Website:	www.mjdistillery.com
Visitor Centre:	Yes
Strength:	45%

This 'urban small-batch distillery' is located – and wait for it, because this may be a first – in a former coffin shop in Hove. That's to say, not Brighton. Coincidentally, the Brighton Gin distillery is a near neighbour, but the two businesses are quite distinct and independent.

It's a boutique-style two-person operation, established in 2018 by Ian and Inger Curtis, life and business partners, who are chemist and biologist respectively. So, proper laboratory-trained scientists, which is a great basis on which to open a distillery. But they are of two minds and had very different ideas on what constitutes a great gin, hence the distillery offering 'The Chemist' (Ian) and 'The Biologist' (that's Inger) as alternative styles.

Far be it from me to come between them, so I thought it best to concentrate on another of their expressions, the Gin of Paradise, which doffs its cap to the grains of paradise spice, first brought to gin prominence by Bombay Sapphire and popping up now in any number of gins. But what you might not know is that in eighteenth-century England it was banned as a dangerous adulteration. In fact, it's still illegal in the state of Florida, leading some opportunistic Miami attorney to sue Bombay's owners Bacardi as recently as September 2019. Apparently, based on an 1868 law, it's believed that grains of paradise can turn otherwise modest and self-effacing drinkers into suicidal madmen driven to give away all their money.

But don't worry. Who are you going to believe – the scientists or a Miami lawyer? Or, indeed, me, because I've tried it, purely in the interests of public safety, you understand, and, to Mrs B.'s considerable relief, still had enough cash for this week's groceries. The coffin shop is the purest coincidence.

So what we have here is the citrus-spice notes of the grains of paradise, complemented by sweet almond, lemon, coriander, orris root and juniper. It's a commendably straightforward approach to botanicals that nods to the more traditional approach that a few botanicals, well deployed, are all that's required to provide both complexity and depth. As a result, and in part due to the higher than standard strength, I can see this working well in classic cocktails. Indeed, the Madame Jennifer website also features the distillery's own Coffee Liqueur and their vodka, the makings of the Espresso Martini, alongside a Limoncello and a tasty-sounding Christmas gin.

HARRIS GIN

Distillery:	The Isle of Harris Distillery, Tarbert, Isle of Harris, Outer Hebrides
Website:	www.harrisdistillery.com
Visitor Centre:	Yes
Strength:	45%

While Fisher's is located on the coast, the striking Isle of Harris Distillery is right on the harbourside in Tarbert. I haven't measured both, but there can't be a great deal of difference in their respective distances from the sea.

I took something of an irreverent tone discussing their marketing in my most recent book *Whiskies Galore!* (it's frightfully good – you should definitely buy a copy) and so, rather than upset them, let's see if we can make up.

Although Harris itself is not easy to get to, pre-Covid it was experiencing a boom in tourism. However, the local economy is fragile, and permanent long-term employment hard to find. The distillery was created, in part at least, to provide well-paid skilled jobs in a sustainable business that could work year-round to produce an internationally appealing product while also benefiting from the influx of affluent visitors. Happily, it seems to be working.

Their single malt whisky is well underway, but that takes a long time to mature and consumes much cash. So, a small Italian gin still was installed and Harris Gin was born. It was an immediate success, partly because of Harris's skilled and experienced marketing and brand management team but mainly because it's very good.

But before we get to that, a word or two on the bottle, which is extremely good-looking and satisfying to hold. There are many pleasing details, including a Latin motto subtly embossed on the base, a simple and elegant label and a chunky wood-and-cork stopper. You won't want to put this in the recycling, and I'd expect a good proportion of the bottles to live on as candle holders or water jugs. There's also a very lovely 35cl Cèilidh Bottle hand-made in ceramic. A maximum of 100 are released each week at no fixed day or time so you have to take pot luck to grab one.

The gin itself begins sweetly, with plenty of juniper, but evolves through citrus notes before herbal and floral flavours emerge and then the *pièce de résistance* – a sweet, complex and beguiling maritime note. This is Harris's *coup de théâtre* – local sugar kelp seaweed, collected by hand by a local diver – and it contributes to making a sensational Martini, because if you like the sugar kelp you can add more using the little bottle and dropper they'll sell you.

Honestly, it's one of my new favourites.

ISLAND GIN

Distillery: Scilly Spirit Distillery, St Mary's Island, Scilly
Website: www.scillyspirit.com
Visitor Centre: Yes
Strength: 44%

Being a land-locked landlubber myself, I assumed that an island would be pretty coastal, so I checked and so it proved. Silly me. In fact, there's a coast all round! Who knew?

Scilly Spirit is a relatively new entrant to the gin market but has already collected an impressive number of major awards, both for its standout packaging and, more importantly, the tasty liquid it contains. Husband-and-wife team Arthur and Hilary Miller established their distillery on St Mary's, the most south-westerly point of the UK in May 2019, aiming to reflect the distinctive nature of their location.

The rather lovely bottle, impressive even by the standards of the global spirits industry, echoes the shape of the Bishop Rock lighthouse with a number of details emphasising Scilly's maritime heritage and using striking aqua-green glass reminiscent of the colour and clarity of the surrounding Atlantic Ocean. The Bishop Rock itself was where, in January 1665, the East Indiaman ship *Royal Oak* of the British East India Company was wrecked while on her first voyage home from the Moluccas, carrying porcelain and peppercorns (incidentally, after a no-doubt disagreeable fifty-two hours marooned on the rocks some of the crew were rescued).

Peppercorns therefore feature as a principal component of the botanicals in Scilly Island, but alongside traditional juniper, plenty of citrus notes, hints of spice and sweet, slightly vegetal fennel. It's classic, no-nonsense gin delivered in some style and at a sensible strength (44%). If you like a little stronger delivery, then explore the depths of their 57% Atlantic Strength, with its tidal waves of flavour.

There's a welcome commitment to environmental good practice and a recognition of the fragility of the pristine island surroundings. Gin is posted in plastic-free packaging; the botanicals are ethically sourced and, once used, either composted or used as animal feed; the distillery has a closed cooling system and is aiming to install solar panels; and an electric van makes local deliveries. Obviously, the bottles can be recycled, but I'd be very surprised if many end up in a skip as they are clearly destined to a second life as elegant candle holders.

All things considered, it's an impressive debut from this far-flung outpost and definitely one to try when you're tired of some of the novelty offerings provided by other fledgling distilleries.

MANLY SPIRITS COASTAL CITRUS

Distillery:	Manly Spirits Co. Distillery, Winbourne Road, Brookvale, Sydney, Australia
Website:	www.manlyspirits.com.au
Visitor Centre:	Yes
Strength:	43%

Described as a combination of 'carefree beach life and urban sophistication', the beachside town of Manly is 'seven miles from Sydney, a thousand miles from care'. Where better to make gin? Founded in April 2017, Manly Spirits undertook intensive research exploring distilleries in the USA, Europe and the UK – and hands-on training in Tasmania, where much of Australia's craft-distilling industry was started.

There's a lot of really interesting, ground-breaking distilling going on right now in Australia, with a brave and innovative new generation challenging orthodoxies and established wisdom, especially in whisky.

Leaving aside whisky and the casual and laid-back vibe, this is a serious and professional operation with four impressive stills, including a substantial 600-litre Holstein still for the distillation of gin and vodka, complemented with a second, smaller 50-litre copper pot still. Working with a chef, they forage marine botanicals, suggesting that the inclusion of these and other Australian native botanicals ensures that their spirits celebrate the uniqueness of these ingredients while attempting to showcase what Australian spirits are all about.

There is also a deep commitment to good environmental practice, clearly explained on their website. They've already developed a full range of gins, all based on Australian wheat spirit. These include Dry, Pink, Barrel Aged and a limited-release Amber Spiced Gin but, partial as I am to citrus flavours, I've picked out their Coastal Citrus Gin (helpfully, it's also called Coastal so it fits in here perfectly). You should find it available from various UK specialists at around £35.

What makes it different? Well, lots of lemony things: lemon aspen, sea parsley, lemon myrtle, fresh coriander leaf and Meyer lemon as well as juniper, of course. The aforementioned marine botanicals are local (the website even provides locations) and gathered with respect for the environment in a sustainable harvest. It's a bright, refreshing gin with a range of intriguing and (to the British palate at least) unusual flavours that it's a shame to drown in too much tonic.

The bottle is fun too, with the Manly Spirits fish logo swimming round the base of the striking blue glass. All things considered, it's an impressive effort from a young company set for further success.

MERMAID GIN

Distillery:	Isle of Wight Distillery, Pondwell Hill, Ryde, Isle of Wight
Website:	www.isleofwightdistillery.com
Visitor Centre:	Mermaid Bar
Strength:	42%

We're all beguiled by the legend of the mermaid. A strange creature, half-woman, half-fish, her sweet singing and alluring appearance lures sailors, princes and pirates to a watery death. They appear in folk mythology from Orkney to Japan, in Homer's *Odyssey* and Hans Christian Andersen's *The Little Mermaid* (sadly, things didn't work out so well for her) and – who could forget? – the movie *Splash* … Daryl Hannah is nice, but I'm not sure if I'd trust a mermaid further than the shallows.

But, as a natural reference point for an island distillery, the Isle of Wight's only distillery has adopted the name for two gins. Given the mermaid's reputation for great beauty, you'd expect pretty stunning packaging, and it doesn't disappoint. In a world of designer bottles, some very lovely indeed, this really does stand out – for the shimmering ice-blue colour of the regular London Dry and the clever textured finish reminiscent of some otherworldly scaly thing. Just like those doomed sailors, you're inexorably drawn closer, though this is one mermaid with whom a liaison on the rocks won't end badly.

As we've noted, there are lots of prizes and awards out there for gins, and Mermaid has collected design plaudits from both the IWSC and the Bartenders' Brand Awards. It certainly has enormous shelf appeal and is satisfyingly tactile. What's more, it comes with positive environmental credentials, as the distillery emphasises its use of ethically sourced local natural ingredients and a commitment to sustainability.

Key to the taste, and inspiration for the name, is rock samphire, known locally as 'mermaid's kiss'. This aromatic succulent clings to the cliffs surrounding the island and marks the high-tide line on its majestic beaches, so, on encountering this, any washed-up shipwrecked mariner stumbling ashore would know themselves safe from drowning. Other local botanicals include Boadicea hops harvested from Ventnor Botanic Gardens and elderflower handpicked from nearby fields. The blushing colour of Mermaid Pink Gin, drier in style than many, comes from Arreton Valley strawberries picked less than ten miles away.

Online reviews seem polarised, awarding either one or five stars for taste, but, like it or loathe it, this will sing on your home bar.

PLYMOUTH

Distillery:	Plymouth Distillery, Plymouth, Devon
Website:	www.plymouthdistillery.com
Visitor Centre:	Yes
Strength:	41.2%

Hello, sailor! Back in 1896, Plymouth Gin was specified in the earliest documented recipe for a Dry Martini (I expect you're shaken but not stirred). Despite the early fame, this grand old brand ended up as a makeweight in a series of corporate deals, passing from hand to hand through a series of uncomprehending and largely uncaring owners. It was probably too small and insignificant for anyone to even notice, and so escaped rationalisation and closure until eventually it came into the hands of Pernod Ricard. They own Beefeater and know and care about gin, though of late their head seems have been turned by their purchase of various smaller and trendier craft brands.

The interesting fact about Plymouth is that while London gin can be produced anywhere (because it's a style), since a court action in the 1880s, Plymouth has only been produced in the city itself. The legal action, against a number of London-based distillers who were selling 'Plymouth' gin, suggests the name itself had some cachet. For some years the brand enjoyed Protected Geographical Origin status in EU law, but the relevant geographical indicator has now lapsed, though production remains firmly at the Plymouth Distillery, formerly a monastery inhabited by Black Friars.

Due perhaps to the soft Dartmoor water, the Plymouth style is somewhat sweeter than the classic London Dry style, possessing deep earthy notes and a wonderfully fresh juniper and lemony bite. It has a slight sweetness due to the selection of botanicals with extraordinary concentration and complexity. No single botanical dominates the overall flavour.

If your taste runs to a stronger tot, try Plymouth's Navy Strength (57%) – a right old ironclad amongst Navy gins, and highly rated by aficionados and top cocktail barmen (OK, mixologists). There was also a very limited release of Mr King's 1842 Recipe (45%), said to be the first in a series of limited edition gins celebrating the history of the distillery. Sadly, little more has been heard of this exciting project.

Beloved of the Royal Navy, especially when served with Angostura bitters as the classic Pink Gin, Plymouth gin is now enjoying something of a revival (which is just as well as our navy now seems to consist of not very much at all) in smarter cocktail bars and amongst gin drinkers looking for something a little offbeat but not so unconventional as might scandalise the vicar.

RAASAY

Distillery:	Isle of Raasay Distillery, Borodale House, Isle of Raasay, Kyle
Website:	www.raasaydistillery.com
Visitor Centre:	Yes
Strength:	46%

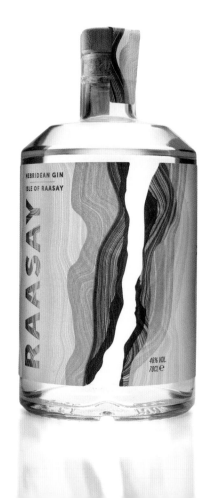

If you ever go over the sea to Skye – rather more prosaically than in the song due to there being a bridge these days – a short drive will take you to the ferry point for Raasay, the agreeable Hebridean island home to a recently opened distillery. The ferry will carry your car, but unless you plan to explore the island, you can travel on foot and walk up to the distillery and visitor centre, which you see clearly as you approach Raasay's modest jetty. Though local Gaelic place-names reflect a heritage of moonshining, this is the first time anyone has distilled anything here legally. It was, as you might expect, built initially to distil single malt whisky, the first batches of which are now coming of age.

There is a great emphasis on sourcing local barley for the whisky and the same philosophy is applied to the production of Isle of Raasay Gin. Because they have larger production facilities than many new distillers, they can make their own neutral grain spirit, and they have taken a firmly traditional approach to their gin, using a limited range of fairly classic and mainstream botanicals.

Their concern to work with as many ingredients as may be found around them led the distillery to work with local botanist Dr Stephen Bungard. He helped identify the Raasay juniper which forms the backbone of the gin, along with the other botanicals: rhubarb root, lemon peel, orange peel, coriander seeds, angelica root, liquorice root, orris root and cubeb pepper.

So don't expect any great revelations here. This is a refreshing, zesty dry gin very much in the mainstream of the gin tradition – the surprise is that gin is distilled here at all.

Though Raasay might seem tricky to get to, the trip is well worth it. Famous visitors in history include Bonnie Prince Charlie (briefly, due to his being on the run from the Duke of Cumberland's troops at the time) and a few years later, James Boswell and Dr Samuel Johnson, who was most impressed, noting that they 'found nothing but civility, elegance and plenty'. It's said that when the *Royal Yacht Britannia* was still in service, the Queen and family would enjoy picnics on Inver Beach to escape the paparazzi.

In fact, *Condé Nast Traveller* magazine rated Raasay one of the 'Best Islands to Visit in 2020' – and not just for the gin.

TAPPERS DARKSIDE COASTAL GIN

Distillery:	Tappers, Champions Business Park, Upton, Wirral, Merseyside
Website:	www.tappersgin.com
Visitor Centre:	No. Tasting Room for events
Strength:	39.6%

Tappers Darkside is not as sinister as it might at first appear: it's the local name for the Wirral Peninsula, home to this rather unusual offering. And don't worry, because they also make a Brightside.

Confused? Well, they're two versions of the same botanical recipe treated with two different production methods and, as such, probably unique. Darkside uses the 'bathtub' method of cold compounding, which essentially means the botanicals have been infused or macerated in the base neutral spirit. Once the mainstay of illicit Prohibition-era production and consequently regarded as an inferior method, associated with cheap or bootleg spirits, here it has been practised with rather greater care and consistency to produce a genuinely different, award-winning gin with an unusual but all-natural amber colour.

By contrast, Brightside is a London Dry. That means all the botanicals go into the still with the base spirit, and no flavouring or colour is added once distillation is complete. This accounts for the fact that Brightside is, indeed, bright (clear and colourless) and bottled at 47% rather than its opposite number's 39.6%.

What's the point of all this? Well, essentially to showcase the difference that a change in production style can make to the same basic ingredients. Founder Dr Steve Tapril launched Tappers in 2016 with the aim of emulating a world of clandestine parties and secret speakeasies with a thoroughly modern approach to compounding.

And, you may well be asking, what, apart from the location, makes it 'coastal'? The answer is provenance. The key botanicals are foraged locally to include sea beet, chickweed and red clover. There's a distinctly brackish note (in a good way, calling to mind ozone on the wind and seaweed lying in hot sun) to Darkside, which drinks fuller than the strength would suggest. It makes a mean Negroni or Old Fashioned where Brightside's natural partner is a quality tonic.

Tappers have not rested on their laurels. They have extended their range with a seasonal range: a distinctly eccentric Easter chocolate gin, Eggcentric, and what they claim to be the UK's first Figgy Pudding Christmas gin. Batches are limited to no more than 100 bottles, all individually filled, labelled, wax-sealed and numbered by hand. For presentation alone, they stand out, but I really love the quiet humour of their distinctive offerings.

IN THE PINK

Whether it's compounded, distilled or a London gin, since December 2008 there have been regulations in place defining gin in both the UK and EU. Without going into the minutiae, what they have to say about the taste of gin is straightforward. They state that the production of all gins must ensure that the taste is predominantly that of juniper berries (*juniperus communis*) with a minimum strength of 37.5% abv.

That seems simple enough, and for years it had been clear anyway: gin had a slightly piney, resinous taste from the juniper, and that was what it tasted like. If you didn't like it, you could drink whisky or brandy, or if you wanted the least possible taste, there was always cheap vodka. 'Pink Gin' (also known as 'gin and bitters') was just that: a simply made and long-established cocktail of gin with a few shakes of Angostura or merely a few drops rinsed around the glass and served very cold.

Then along came some upstart 'Pink Gins' – that is to say, gins which were pink in colour but not derived from Angostura or other bitters and not sold as a pre-mixed version of the classic cocktail. They were, in fact, gins which were pink (or related shades) in colour, with the reddish flush coming from berries. These might be raspberries, strawberries or even blackberries – it didn't seem to matter. Now, one might look somewhat pedantically at that development, arguing that Pink Gin already existed and that these new products would have been better described as 'Flavoured Gins' or even 'Spirit Drinks'. That's a catch-all legal descriptor for spirits which don't fall into the conventional classifications and, as with at least some of these products it was stretching matters to describe the taste as being predominantly of juniper, there was a case to be made that these weren't really, truly gins. But as there's no definitive way to determine whether or not a taste is 'predominantly' juniper, that meant there was a loophole in the regulations. And wherever there's a loophole, there will be some ingenious folk ready to exploit it.

And, as by 2015 gin was back in fashion and well on the way to becoming sexy as a name – which Spirit Drink never will be – the consumer, who eagerly embraced these essentially frivolous creations, was not to be denied. Setting aside their reservations (if indeed they had any), more and more producers – first the smaller distillers, then increasingly the large brands – decided to capitalise on the opportunity. If it looked as if it might be a short-lived fashion, they could always claim it was a 'small-batch' or, better still, a 'limited edition'.

As I write, though, it looks as if this is very much not the case, and Pink Gin, twenty-first-century style, is here to stay, at least for the foreseeable future. Major well-established brands, who perhaps would have looked askance at all this even ten years ago, have now launched their own versions. Today, for example, even staid old Gordon's offer 'the natural sweetness of raspberries and strawberries with the tang of redcurrant served up in a unique blushing tone' as Gordon's Premium Pink. To be fair, juniper remains evident, but even though they claim it is derived from an 1880s recipe, I suspect that the original Alexander Gordon might share the blushes. Amongst the other leading brands we find Tanqueray Blackcurrant Royale, Bombay Bramble, the limited edition Hendrick's Midsummer and, not to be outdone, Beefeater Pink Strawberry and Peach & Raspberry gins.

However, in defence of all the above, the history books do confirm that flavoured gins were not unknown in the past. Old Tom, for example, a style popular with Victorian drinkers but now being energetically rediscovered as a key ingredient in certain cocktails, was a sweetened gin. The Gordon's version, Special Old Tom, hung around until 1987, and Gordon's produced Orange Gin (1929) and a Lemon Gin (1931), though, in the more recent nadir of gin, both had been discontinued by 1990. So, there is a respectable argument that, with these new expressions, gin is rediscovering a lost past – not that heritage appears to overly concern very many of today's drinkers.

Once the horse had bolted, there was little to stop the more experimentally minded distiller launching his or her own increasingly outlandish style of flavoured gin, possibly as a genuine exploration of flavour, though sometimes it's hard to avoid the suspicion that some were novelties dreamt up in search of publicity (thank you, social media). You might even think, with apologies to Taylor Swift, that because they're young and reckless, they take this way too far. But there's nothing to fear: choosing the wrong flavoured gin might leave you breathless, but there's no danger of a scar, other than to your credit card.

A quick trawl of smaller brands' websites quickly reveals Apple Crumble Gin, Rhubarb & Custard Gin, several Marmalade Gins, multiple versions of Christmas Gin, Papaya & Ginger Gin, Baked Apple & Salted Caramel Gin, Haggis, Neeps & Tatties Gin, Nettle Gin, Lemon Drizzle Gin, Quince Gin, Hop Gin, Truffle Gin, and so on. Much as I would like to suggest that I have tried all these in the interests of my research, I would be misleading you – frankly, you're on your own with some of them, fun though they sound. Indeed, full disclosure: I may have made one of these up. See if you can guess which is the imposter, though there's more than an outside chance that someone will have taken the idea, quite bizarre though it is, and launched it. Look out for an announcement next 25 January (that's a hint, btw).

Reassuringly, Pangolin Gin is not made from the curiously endearing but threatened termite-chomping, scaly mammal found in Asia and Africa. The same applies to Elephant Gin – no animals are harmed in the making of these two gins and, in fact, both donate from their sales to conservation efforts helping their namesakes. There are not forty-seven simians in Monkey 47 Gin – not even one. However, for a mere £199 a bottle you can buy Anty Gin, which is made, as the name would suggest, with real ants (of the red-wood variety) – a strangely precise sixty-two of the little fellas in every bottle, from which we may deduce that a good number of insects were harmed in the making. You're *definitely* on your own with that one.

It is possible to feel that the lure of the G-word has been exploited with a little too much enthusiasm and that an excess of entrepreneurial flair has led us to some very strange places: gin-soaked chocolates and preserves; GIN on every item of clothing imaginable; in lip balm, candles and on 'inspirational' posters and even on cushions. At Christmas there are gin-filled baubles to hang on the tree, which seems like a fire risk to me, though I daresay Mr & Mrs S. Claus are grateful.

More worryingly, there has been a trend recently for drinks labelled as gin, or suggesting gin is a key ingredient, but from which the spirit is sadly completely absent. The Gin Guild, a trade body, has been active in challenging misleading labelling such as 'Alcohol Free Gin & Tonic', with not a trace of gin, and a 1.2% abv juniper spirit known as 'CleanGin'. Both have been withdrawn, but similar products continue to pop up, clutching gin's coat tails. So beware, there are deceptive products out there, superficially alluring but sham and pallid imitations of the real thing. Naturally, none are featured within these pages.

Before looking in detail at a few pink and flavoured gins, it's perhaps worth noting that there is a kind of logic behind some of these apparently weird and wonderful flavours. Various citrus botanicals are used in many gins, and, personally speaking, I am rather partial to a citrus note on the palate. Hence Lemon Drizzle Gin (Sipsmith), Marmalade Gins (Chase, Slingsby, Zymurgorium Manchester and others too many to toast), Tanqueray Flor de Sevilla, Lind & Lime (Port of Leith) and others in this vein are merely emphasising something that's genuinely there in the first place and, incidentally, does no harm in a number of cocktails. By the same token, the use of berries is not so great a stretch, as once again their role is to emphasise flavour notes that are inherent in some botanicals.

Let's explore a few pink and flavoured gins that offer a welcome variety and note of gaiety to counteract any tendency to take gin too seriously – but, casting caution to the winds and departing from my normal alphabetical order, let's first consult an expert and start with a proper Pink Gin to remind us what this is all about.

PROPER PINK

Distillery:	That Boutique-y Gin Company (Master of Malt)
Website:	www.thatboutiqueygincompany.com
Visitor Centre:	No
Strength:	46%

'The Expert liked the Glock 19M, which particularly for close-range work is a professional's gun. At 7.5 grams the 9x19 mm Parabellum round has an impact energy of 600 joules with a typical muzzle velocity of 1,400 feet per second. The round had less than 12 feet to travel before entering Morgan's temple. An aerosol of blood, bone and brain matter sprayed the wall hangings as he spun round and fell. French, he'd said, probably seventeenth-century. They'd clean though and as the instructors at the Depot had stressed time and again: take the shot you get and leave quietly and calmly. It was good advice. The Expert should have followed it.'

Admit it. I've got your attention now. And you should pay attention to this puppy because it's Proper Pink Gin. Not only does it say so on the label, but it has a picture of a Leading Expert (he even has a badge that says it, so it has to be true) blowing a raspberry. Why? Because there are no raspberries in this. This is a berry-free zone.

The Boutique-y Gin Company, a specialist bottler of many wonderful things, have made this as a proper Pink Gin, that is to say a simple pre-mixed bottle of gin and Angostura bitters, at a proper 46%. The End.

I'm more than a little worried about the 'Expert', though. He seems to be wearing a naval uniform which puts me in mind of 007, Commander James Bond himself. Though he would likely never have used the Glock (being suspicious of its Austrian manufacturer for one thing), as a one-time Royal Naval officer he would have been more than familiar with the Pink Gin, very much the default call in many a wardroom. And he did like the odd libation.

He does drink it in Ian Fleming's final novel *The Man with the Golden Gun*. As Fleming writes, 'The red-coated barman asked him what he would have and he said, "Some pink gin. Plenty of bitters. Beefeater's." There was desultory talk about the relative merits of gins. Everyone else seemed to be drinking champagne except Mr Hendriks, who stood away from the group and nursed a Schweppes Bitter Lemon.'

Several mysteries here, then. Did KGB agent Hendriks inspire a brand of gin? Does Proper Pink contain Beefeater? This calls for a Leading Expert …

ABER FALLS ORANGE MARMALADE

Distillery:	Aber Falls, Abergwyngregyn, North Wales
Website:	www.aberfallsdistillery.com
Visitor Centre:	Yes
Strength:	41.3%

There are a few really expensive gins out there, not least because there's thought to be a certain promotional kudos attached to being 'the most expensive gin in [insert location here]'. I get a lot of breathless press releases like this from over-excited PR types and tend to resist them, but even in the world of very high prices, the £1,085 paid for a single bottle of Aber Falls Summit Gin: Mountaineers Cut stands head and shoulders above most.

Although this was mainly created to generate some media coverage – it's not every day that gin is distilled in a copper pot still on top of Snowdon, the highest mountain in England and Wales at 1,085 metres, so I hope you spotted the link to the price – funds from the online auction went to the Wales Air Ambulance charity, to keep their helicopters flying. There were only three bottles produced and it's a deserving cause, so I think it deserves a mention.

This relatively new distillery was set up to make Welsh whisky, the first batches of which have recently been released, but by late 2017 Aber Falls entered the gin market. Their distilling creativity more than matches their ingenious publicity strategies and they now offer a tight range of four gins, including Welsh Dry and the more premium Small Batch, which is apparently 'inspired by ancient flavours that date back to Druid times'. Let's hope they kept their distiller well clear of the magic mushrooms …

So far as anyone knows, the ancient Druids never made marmalade (the Marmelet of Oranges recipe is attributed to one Eliza Cholmondeley from around 1677), so although they may have been top banana amongst the Celts, they would have had no idea what to do with a bag of oranges. [Enough fruit jokes – Ed.]

Why don't you try an Aber Falls Yummy Mummy? (I'd just like to make it clear that's their title, not mine. Don't blame me and don't write in.) To continue: 30ml Aber Falls Orange Marmalade Gin, 10ml orange bitters, freshly squeezed lemon juice and elderflower cordial to top up, with a slice of dried orange as a garnish.

For a full-size bottle and at 41.3% strength the Aber Falls flavoured range (there are rhubarb and ginger variants too) offers excellent value. One tricky thing, though: two bottles don't quite bring your online shopping basket to the free shipping threshold. Problems, problems – that can only mean a third bottle.

BEAUFORT
FIFTY-SEVEN

Distillery:	Langley, Warley and Union Distillers, Market Harborough
Website:	www.beaufortspirit.com
Visitor Centre:	No
Strength:	57%

This is a rather complex and most unusual product, which collected a rare Gold Outstanding award in the IWSC's Contemporary Gin category in 2020. There are very few Gold Outstanding medals presented, and as the IWSC is one of the more rigorous and demanding award schemes, this alone demands your attention.

The punchy 57% abv strength and designation of 'Smoked Sipping Gin' further mark this out as very different from run-of-the-mill gins. It's the singular creation of Leo Crabtree, founder of the BeauFort London fragrance house, working with Langley Distillery, who create the gin base, and the Halen Môn smokery in Anglesey, source of the smoked water which is then blended with the high-strength spirit by Union Distillers of Leicestershire. Incidentally, the Halen Môn water will set you back £4.40 for a 10cl bottle so don't go spilling any!

The name 'Beaufort' of course brings to mind a connection to the Royal Navy, that of Rear Admiral Francis Beaufort, inventor of the Beaufort Scale – the first standardised measurement of wind speeds which, somewhat refined, remains in use to the present day. The strength of 57% was inspired, however, by the creation story of Navy gin – that gunpowder soaked in spirit at this strength would still blow up, thus confirming the liquid's 'proof'. But whether this curious gin causes you to explode or simply makes waves it's certainly thought-provoking and stands out for that.

The smoked water on its own is complemented by an unusual mix of botanicals. Alongside the conventional juniper, coriander, angelica root, orange and lemon peel, orris and liquorice we encounter Sichuan pepper and pink pepper with smoked oak and hickory chips – as far as I'm aware, unique to this gin. There's more citrus than you might expect on initial impressions, but then clouds of smoke gather, eventually giving way to the delicious spices. Overall, it's an impressive creation, testimony to a determinedly different approach.

Just as the product is outside the mainstream, so the packaging sets it apart with an authoritative, heavy, square glass bottle and solid pewter label. It's not a gin that you'll want to drink a lot of at any one time, and perhaps not every day; it's something to keep for more mindful drinking or for experimentation in some offbeat cocktails that will intrigue even blowhard gin snobs (you know who you are).

CHASE PINK GRAPEFRUIT & POMELO

Distillery:	Chase Distillery, Rosemaund Farm, Hereford
Website:	www.chasedistillery.co.uk
Visitor Centre:	Yes
Strength:	40%

I've mentioned Chase's excellent Elegant 48 Gin elsewhere in this book. Now part of Diageo, they represent the entrepreneurial success story of Herefordshire potato farmer William Chase, who was quick to appreciate the opportunity in craft spirits back in 2008.

One of the things that makes them stand out is their extensive range of flavoured gins, which includes Pink Grapefruit & Pomelo, Rhubarb & Bramley Apple, Seville Marmalade, Hedgerow Elderflower and Oak Aged Sloe gins. Quite apart from launching their products early, in recognition of the renewed interest in gin, Chase shrewdly saw the possibilities of (then) unconventional flavours. New drinkers taking an interest in gin were not constrained by tradition or preconceptions of what gin should taste like. Freed from any brand legacy, Chase were able to bring an entirely fresh perspective to the market and offer new expressions that new drinkers were more than willing to explore.

Nowadays, there is nothing *outré* or particularly contrived about the range, which seems to me to reflect gin's traditions with bottling at 40% and products that are recognisably gin but with certain key flavour notes emphasised. Many of the botanicals used – grapefruit, limes, orange peels and elderflower – will be found in any number of other more conventional gins; it's simply that there are more of them here. But, rest assured, gin's essential juniper keynote is never missing in action.

The distillery stresses its field-to-bottle operation, and because of the farm's location, waste products are usefully employed as fertiliser or cattle feed, and the steam energy used to run the distillery is produced on site from a biomass boiler powered by prunings from their apple orchard. The scale of the operation means that Chase can make their own neutral spirit on site – the basis of their vodka and the start of the gin which can truly claim to have been made from scratch. The copper pot still, Ginny, used for gin production incorporates a Carterhead chamber with botanicals added both into the body of the still and the gin basket, according to the individual recipe.

So, what we have here are fresh, clean contemporary interpretations of an English classic which work well in a simple G&T or provide a jumping-off point for a range of cocktails (there are some helpful suggestions on the website). It's little surprise that Diageo came calling.

JAFFA CAKE

Distillery:	Zesty Spirits (Master of Malt)
Website:	www.jaffacakegin.com
Visitor Centre:	No
Strength:	42%

Sounds bonkers, doesn't it? And indeed that was my first reaction. But I should know better. The folks at Zesty Spirits (or perhaps that's Master of Malt, or Atom Brands, I never know – but they're all gathered under the same umbrella, so I'm not sure it matters) bring us all kind of off-the-wall but very tasty things. I've enjoyed their Proper Pink Gin and recall the Citrol London Dry with great fondness.

Generally speaking, they tend to be short-run, experimental releases that come and go in a burst of enthusiasm that, while perhaps appearing irreverent or sometimes downright daft, are underpinned by real love for the spirits industry and an appreciation of how drinks work and how we use them. Think of it as two timeless classics together, and, let's be honest, who doesn't love a Jaffa Cake with their gin? I know I do (well, maybe with my morning coffee).

However, you might easily dismiss this as a bit of a gimmick and assume it to be rather sickly-sweet tasting – more of a liqueur than a gin. But that's where you'd be wrong, because despite the garish packaging, jokey copy and apparently silly idea what we have here – once you've accepted gins that move off a strict juniper base just a little bit – is a perfectly fine product. It tastes, as you might expect, uncommonly like a Jaffa Cake, with tangy oranges, sweet vanilla and almonds, and hints of dark chocolate, but still with juniper in there to placate the purists.

In fact, Orange Gins were a thing until comparatively recently and old bottles do turn up on auction sites – more of a curiosity, I'd say, than anything you'd want to drink, as the product stability of a 30- or 40-year-old bottle can't be relied upon. So, think of this as a salute to gin's heritage if that makes it easier, but I'm comfortably certain that you'll be convinced within the first couple of glasses, after which you'll begin to appreciate the potential here for a cocktail or three.

The most obvious use will be in a Negroni, but Jaffa Cake Gin will add a burst of citrus, with some underlying complexity from the vanilla, almonds and chocolate, to almost any gin-based cocktail. And, by small-batch distillery standards, it's modestly enough priced for a full-size bottle. With change from £30 for a packet of something tasty, it's a case of having your cake and eating it.

KYRÖ PINK

Distillery:	Isokyrö, Finland
Website:	www.kyrodistillery.com
Visitor Centre:	Yes
Strength:	38.2%

Founded as recently as 2014 by five friends in a sauna, Kyrö enjoyed unexpected worldwide success when its first gin, Napue (now simply branded Kyrö), won the IWSC's inaugural Gin and Tonic Trophy in 2015. The IWSC is one of the few award schemes really worth taking note of and, consequently, sales exploded. But it was all something of a surprise as the distillery had been established to make whisky, with gin as something of a sideline to generate some cash while the whisky matured.

Since that early, high-profile win, the business has gone on to considerable success, backed by heavy investment that has allowed them to greatly expand production. Finnish distilling in general has come a long, long way in the last decade and there are now some very impressive products emerging from the land of larch and lakes. Kyrö's whisky in particular lives up to their gin's award-winning standard.

There's a great sense of irreverence around Kyrö, and while the partners take their work seriously, they are not slow to poke fun at themselves as a quick glance at their website or promotional videos will reveal. Their take on Pink Gin is a little offbeat, but whether or not it lives up to their claim that it is 'a celebration of true equality in taste, people & thoughts', I will leave it to you to decide.

For my money, that would be a bold aspiration for the Nobel Peace Prize, let alone a bottle of gin, but I suppose sharing a bottle might bring two warring factions to at least a temporary cessation of hostilities. It's remarkable what some mindfully foraged lingonberries, strawberries and rhubarb (a popular choice for flavoured gins) can do. The natural ingredients give this a delicate pink colour that may fade over time – not that this will be a problem, as I don't see a bottle lasting long once opened.

It's worth noting as you are poised over the 'buy' button that the bottle is the smaller 50cl size and the strength a little on the low side at 38.2%, making this not quite the bargain it may first appear. Allowing for the smaller volume and lower strength, you'd pay close to £40 for a full-size, full-strength bottle. Don't hold back, though; this is quite the treat.

LUXARDO
SOUR CHERRY

Distillery:	Giralamo Luxardo, Torreglia, Padua, Italy
Website:	www.luxardo.it
Visitor Centre:	Shop at distillery
Strength:	37.5%

Luxardo are a long-established and highly respected Italian drinks company who also make those jars of fantastic Maraschino cherries – fabulous for cocktails and adding great depth of flavour to a rich fruit cake.

In a world of bland corporate giants, they remain in the hands of the founding family and, in 2021, celebrated their 200th anniversary. Sadly, the impressive original distillery was destroyed during the Second World War (there are some fascinating pictures on the website), but the family was able to restart operations in Torreglia, near Padua, where they grow their Marasca Luxardo cherries, the foundation of the family's fortunes and the company's success.

Until recently, they were best known for their Maraschino Originale and Sangue Morlacco or Morlacco Blood, the name coined by the famous Italian poet Gabriele D'Annunzio, who was an enthusiast for this intensely sweet yet tart liqueur. So, total destruction of their distillery apart, life has been a bowl of cherries for the Luxardo family, who have expanded their gin offering with this Sour Cherry variant.

Unlike some, they are not coming late to the gin party, having prepared juniper-based distillates since 1833 and offered their Ginepro di Dalmazia from the early 1900s. Today, they produce an Italian London Dry style which is the base for this Sour Cherry style, first released in summer 2018.

It's one of the very few sour cherry gins in the world. Actually, come to think of it, I can't name another one, but someone else must surely be using this versatile fruit. While the colour is unexpected, the taste is quite the revelation. This is not a sloe-gin-style liqueur but a real gin at full strength, albeit with a very different twist. The initially forceful nose gives way on the palate to a well-balanced combination of slightly tannic, almost woody, sour cherry with plenty of ripe fruit, almonds, spice and juniper notes.

The company suggest it could be used to twist many classic cocktails such as the Martinez and the Gin Fizz, or in a Cherry Gin Sour, and I can imagine it becoming a mixologist's favourite. Unfortunately for Luxardo, the arrival of the Covid pandemic badly affected trade, disrupting the early adoption of Sour Cherry. However, it really stands out from the mass of flavoured gins and offers something distinctive and genuinely new that's destined to bloom in time.

MARY-LE-BONE ORANGE & GERANIUM

Distillery:	The Pleasure Gardens Distilling Company, 108 Marylebone Lane, London
Website:	www.marylebonegin.com
Visitor Centre:	108 Brasserie
Strength:	46.2%

This is another adventure in gin from Johnny Neill (see Whitley Neill), who has set up Isabella, a remarkably small but lovely still, in the confines of the 108 Brasserie, Marylebone. That makes it London's most centrally located distillery and one of the smallest you are ever likely to see, certainly while contemplating the pleasures of the £38 Grass-fed 170g Hereford fillet steak, with peppercorn sauce and fries. The perfect distillery visitor centre in fact.

As the faux-Victorian label makes clear, the Mary-Le-Bone gins are inspired by the pleasure gardens once popular with all of London society – and other less refined patrons. In the eighteenth century, Marylebone was on London's rural edge and thus ideally located for a pleasure garden. These outdoor entertainment spaces were first popularised in the 1730s and rapidly acquired a reputation for their unique combination of fashionable entertainment, music, food and drink combined with sexual intrigue, enthusiastic consumption of alcohol and a thrilling sense of danger. The modest admission fee of sixpence may have deterred the lowest class of prostitute and pickpocket, but part of the pleasure garden's clandestine appeal was the frisson of ever-present menace. Described by the Museum of London as 'simultaneously an art gallery, a restaurant, a brothel, a concert hall and a park', the nearest modern equivalent is probably Soho in its post-war bohemian heyday.

Naturally, like Soho, gin was an essential element of the pleasure garden, and as befits his reputation as one of the most innovative of distillers, Johnny Neill has created the Pleasure Gardens Distilling Company to produce limited runs of very special gins.

I know that awards aren't necessarily the alpha and omega guiding all judgement, but since March 2018 when Isabella was revealed, Mary-Le-Bone gins have been gathering exceptional plaudits in major competitions. This Orange & Geranium style was declared the World's Best Flavoured Gin in 2020, and I will confess to my complete shock and surprise on receiving a bottle from the affable Mr Neill. Not, I quickly add, at his generosity but at the gin's vibrant colour which, alarmingly, resembles Irn-Bru, the carbonated beverage of choice in Scotland. It was a disconcerting moment. But I advise you to ignore your initial disquiet, savour its frightfully curious botanical wonderment and dive into a whole new world of sweet orange ginny pleasure – a taste of a lost demi-monde.

TANQUERAY BLACKCURRANT ROYALE

Distillery:	Diageo Cameronbridge Distillery, Leven, Fife
Website:	www.tanqueray.com
Visitor Centre:	No
Strength:	41.3%

Strange to relate, Tanqueray is actually made in Scotland, right next door to the stills used to make Gordon's because both are part of the Diageo empire, and although the brand is the epitome of London, it's actually a bigger seller in the USA than in its home market.

It's something of a surprise to see a brand this traditional embrace the trend for flavoured gins, but like Granddad dancing at a wedding, Tanqueray has done so with considerable verve, releasing not one but three variants: Rangur (lime); Flor de Sevilla (orange) and now the Blackcurrant Royale (blackcurrant, obvs). This reflects the strong American bias in their sales and distribution; flavoured vodkas have been a phenomenon in that market, and cocktail culture has entered the mainstream to a greater extent there than almost anywhere, due in part to the Covid pandemic. All three work very well, not least because they're bottled at 41.3%. That's a little weaker than standard Tanqueray and its big brother No. Ten but higher than the majority of flavoured gins, making it better value than many others, delivering a more satisfying mouth feel and offering more punch once mixed.

The claim is that Blackcurrant Royale was inspired by Charles Tanqueray's travels to France, though it might just have more to do with changing customer tastes. That said, it's made with the four botanicals of Tanqueray London Dry Gin and then blended with French blackcurrants, vanilla and black orchid, which add the 'exotic floral notes' found when tasted neat.

For the most part, however, this will find its way into various cocktails, presumably with a blackcurrant garnish. One idea would be to add a splash of prosecco or to use this as the base for a quick and easy Bramble. You can always persuade yourself of the alleged health benefits of the humble blackcurrant, said to be bursting with vitamin C (N.B. this does *not* constitute health or dietary advice).

It's rather a disappointment that there's no public access to the distillery, which is part of a much larger and inevitably rather industrial complex, but there's plenty to enjoy in Tanqueray's flavoured range. It is a great testament to the distilling team's creativity and imagination. These new styles were initially launched on an experimental basis, but such has been the positive response that it seems they are now a permanent addition. I imagine that Charles Tanqueray would approve.

COOL
COCKTAILS

Say what you like about pandemics and lockdowns but they're great for stimulating cocktail making at home. And, while DIY bartending may have removed some of the mystique (and a certain amount of mumbo-jumbo into the bargain), the main effect has been to encourage experimentation, which has been great for online sales of gin and the various other ingredients that some recipes call for. Silver linings and all that for the cenosillicaphobic amongst us.

So we started with the **Quarantini**, of course, employing the classic formula of equal measures of anything you have in the house; served with or without a mixer, as available; over ice (or not if some domestic crisis calls for especially rapid consumption). Shaken or stirred and with a garnish of anything in the fruit bowl. Paper umbrella optional.

However, we can do better, and I wanted to offer some cool classics together with a couple of contemporary cocktails that you can easily put together at home, without needing to buy lots of obscure ingredients that you'll use only once. So nothing here requires agave syrup, mustard seeds, gochujang (I don't even know what that is and can't be bothered to look it up) or a dusting of matcha green tea powder, none of which anybody keeps at home but all of which appear in various recipes recommended by expert mixologists. Anybody might think they were trying to put you off.

You can go online to buy the various bits of equipment you'll see used in proper bars but, until you get the hang of mixing your own and decide they're vital, most kitchen cupboards should have all you need, other than fancy glassware (and unless you're trying to impress the neighbours, and I'm not sure that matters all that much). Let's face it, sitting in front of Netflix your creation would taste pretty much the same out of a jam jar.

To start off with I worked with Craig Harper of Fever-Tree to create a couple of simple but delicious serves that are easy to prepare and even easier to drink. Full disclosure: I say 'worked with' but, in truth, Craig did the work and I sat around, tried different samples and made more-or-less approving noises until a final formula was agreed. I told him I liked citrus-led tastes and had a bit of a sweet tooth and he came up with these.

Buxton's Bucket of Blood

This is a orange-y twist on the **Bramble** (which we'll meet in greater detail shortly).

35ml gin (of your choice, but read on . . .)
15ml bramble liqueur
Serve with Fever-Tree Italian Blood Orange Soda, over ice and garnished with a blackberry and an orange wedge

As regards the gin, I'd suggest a classic London Dry. To dial up the citrus impact you could use Tanqueray's Rangpur or Flor de Sevilla which offer more lime or bitter orange notes respectively.

For the liqueur, Craig recommends The Braemble Gin Liqueur, which is made with a combination of London Dry gin and Scottish blackberries (the best, trust me on this). This was created by Craig along with Mike Aikman and Jason Scott from Edinburgh's brilliant Bramble Bar. As he says, 'other crème de mûres are available' and you will have to order this specially, but it's not expensive and once the bottle arrives you'll find there are plenty of other ways to enjoy it. In fact, you'll soon need another.

You can pack your glass with ice cubes, but crushed ice looks great. Lacking a machine, how we do that here is by placing regular ice cubes in a clean tea towel and bashing them with something hard. It's not how they do it in the top bars, but see my irreverent thoughts on glassware. In fact, top bar consultant Salvatore Calabrese agrees, telling the Master of Malt blog, 'You don't need lots of equipment to make good drinks – make use of what you have in your house.' Lacking a shaker, he used a jar – you read it here first. Well, second actually.

Granny's Ruin

Like many in the drinks world, Craig and I have noticed that sherry is no longer something your granny drinks at Christmas and then keeps until the next year. The best sherries are amongst the finest and most complex wines in the world and yet still represent excellent value. Pedro Ximénez is a classic style: intensely dark, rich and very, very sweet. It's like drinking an alcoholic concentrate of very ripe Flame raisins. You might sip a glass after dinner as an alternative to port but, on its own, a little goes quite a long way. In the right cocktail, though, it transforms the drink and you can find it in half bottle sizes easily enough, minimizing any risk that you don't like it (you will, though – and if you don't your granny certainly will).

> 35ml London Dry gin
> 15ml Pedro Ximénez
> Serve with Fever-Tree Italian Blood Orange Soda, over ice and garnish with orange and thyme

Again, just go with the gin you like (or have got in the cupboard) but don't stint on the sherry. I've been using El Candado from Valdespino.

So that's two bespoke cocktails specially created for *The Ultimate Companion*. You can't say we don't give you value.

Bramble

Of course, the classic Bramble cannot be ignored. This was first created by the late Dick Bradsell (1959–2016), a giant on the London cocktail scene, with an international reputation. Unless you work in the drinks trade, you will probably have never heard of him, but his work has almost certainly changed the way you drink. We owe to him the invention of the Espresso Martini, the Russian Spring Punch and a number of other modern classics, but for me his stand-out creation has to be the **Bramble**, not least because, unlike the first two mentioned, it's made with gin where they use vodka (but you can use gin – no one's looking).

As the story goes, Bradsell came up with the idea in 1984, later relating that 'I was back in my childhood on the Isle of Wight, going blackberrying, and being pricked by the brambles, […] I had all of this in mind, and I thought, "I want to design a British cocktail."' What he came up with is an absolute classic though curiously he used blackcurrant liqueur which, rather pedantically, I must point out is not the same thing.

50ml London Dry gin
30ml freshly squeezed lemon juice
12.5ml simple syrup (you can buy these ready-made, but it's just an equal mix of sugar and water)
12.5ml blackcurrant liqueur

To serve it correctly, and for the maximum visual appeal, mix the first three ingredients over ice and pour them over a cone-shaped mound of crushed ice, then slowly drizzle the blackcurrant so it seems to seep into the ice. Bradsell garnished with a raspberry, but only because that's what he could get in 1984. A slice of lemon works fine or a bramble itself would be quite apt. Why not?

For the liqueur, dig out that bottle of Braemble you bought earlier; be purist about your **Bramble** and use real blackberry liqueur. However, for further evidence of the great man's confusion, and this may surprise you, Bradsell himself suggested that Ribena would do at a pinch. Being charitable, even the immortals improvise when necessary.

Since the invention of this drink there have been any number of variants. One that pleases me, not least because Bradsell was a huge fan of Bombay Sapphire, uses the recently developed Bombay Bramble, which they say is made with a unique infusion process that capturing the natural flavours of freshly harvested blackberries and raspberries. As well as a fresher, more natural taste this greatly reduces the gin's sugar content which will please our increasingly bossy Health and Safety czars.

50ml Bombay Bramble
25ml freshly squeezed lemon juice
20ml sugar syrup (Bombay suggest a 2:1 ratio)
lemon wedge and raspberries/blackberries x 2 to garnish
Mix and pour over crushed ice

Negroni

Another classic which is a great favourite in this house. It never fails to please.

It's said that this was first created in Florence just after the First World War when Count Camillo Negroni asked the bartender Forsco Scarselli, to strengthen his favourite cocktail – the Americano – by replacing the soda water with gin. It's so straightforward as to be laughable (in retrospect, at the time it was a revelation) but, if you've never tried it before be aware that it's strong and bitter – which is rather the point. It's simply equal 1/3 parts

London Dry gin
sweet (red) vermouth
Campari
Stir together and serve with an orange peel garnish over cubed ice.
   Two are probably enough

But this is where the fun starts, because you can play many tunes on this basic recipe. Note that the quality of the vermouth plays quite a large part. Out of the more easily available vermouths I favour Noilly Prat and am particularly fond of their Ambré. If you don't mind paying a little more, then Italy offers some outstanding possibilities, especially Cucielo Rosso or, for special occasions, Vermouth di Torino Superiore del Professore with its base of vintage Barolo wine.

Entire books have been written about the Negroni. One of the best, simply titled *The Negroni* was by an English cocktail writer, consultant and sometime barman Gary Regan (1951–2019) who was a huge influence on the US cocktail bar scene. He gives a number of recipes for variant Negronis, including this one, which he credits to an unknown young German lady who presented it during a Munich cocktail competition (sadly, the date and her name are not recorded). Regan was so impressed that he named it **Negroni Hors Pair** (in acknowledgement of her peerless talent) and recorded the recipe as follows. Note that it uses American measures – 1 ounce is equivalent to 30ml, so this makes a generous amount.

1 ounce Beefeater 24
1 ounce Taylor Fladgate 20-year-old port
1 ounce Campari
4 dashes 15-year-old balsamic vinegar (made from Pedro
   Ximénez grapes)
Garnish with an orange wheel and a square piece of lemon zest
   (I don't know why it has to be square, perhaps it's a German
   thing), served over ice

Now, I don't suppose you have a bottle of 20-year-old port lying around, and 15-year-old balsamic vinegar may be a challenge, but it's the idea behind this that really interests me. You could experiment with a more everyday Ruby port (e.g. Port of Leith), and most supermarkets will stock a few balsamic vinegars, which are a useful addition to any kitchen (some people apparently even drink it neat).

For a fun twist you could try using Jaffa Cake Gin in your Negroni. When I first heard about this I did wonder if small batch gin hadn't experienced a jump-the-shark moment. I mean, really, gin made with Jaffa Cakes. As the team behind it say: 'Right, we could eat these yummy Jaffa cakes, or we could put the Jaffa cakes in this vacuum still and make Jaffa Cake Gin.'

So that's what they did. The result is as you might expect – gin with marmalade orange and chocolate flavours. Perfect, in fact, for a Negroni that you could serve with a straight face to the hipster in your life. And it works better than you might imagine.

Equal parts Jaffa Cake Gin, Campari and sweet vermouth. Then, as they say, 'whack a Jaffa Cake on the edge of your glass like a citrus wheel. The latter won't exactly add to the drink, but it's guaranteed to make you smile.'

Incidentally, Jaffa Cakes are legally cakes, not biscuits. That's the law, as determined by a 1991 VAT tribunal and, breaking news, they now also come in pineapple flavour. I thought I'd done quite well during the pandemic until I realised that the launch of pineapple flavour Jaffa Cakes was the second most exciting thing that happened to me in 2020 (and, believe me, you don't want to know what was number one).

There are a number of excellent marmalade- or orange-influenced gins available. One in particular that springs to mind is Zymurgorium Manchester Marmalade (see pp. 200–01), because it's delicious but also for the funky name and cool bottle. But spread yourself – other marmalade gins are available.

The Zest of Times

The mention of orange marmalade reminds me of a homemade cocktail I offer to those who share my predilection for citrus flavours. A batch of marmalade was made that didn't set quite satisfactorily. It proved a useful ingredient in cooking meat dishes, then my son Gerry got hold of it and I give you here his **Zest of Times** cocktail.

50ml London Dry gin
50ml freshly squeezed orange juice
egg white
2 teaspoons orange marmalade (not quite set homemade
   marmalade is good)
2–3 dashes orange bitters
Take equal measures of gin and freshly squeezed orange juice; add
   egg white, the marmalade and a couple of dashes of orange bitters.
   Shake, strain to remove the bits of peel (or leave them if you like,
   it's your drink) and serve over ice, with a twist of orange peel as
   garnish. Enjoy!

Gin 'n' Jam

Staying with slightly frivolous, easy to make at home cocktails, the
Gin 'n' Jam from Pinkster might appeal. Pinkster was one of the
early trendsetters in the pink and flavoured gin category. They use
real raspberries to create the gin and then (you may not be surprised
to know this when you learn that the company was founded by an
accountant) use the gin-soaked fruit as the basis for their Gin Jam.
You can enjoy this on your toast, of course, but they suggest it as an
ingredient in their very own cocktail. It's simple enough:

50ml Pinkster
10ml lemon juice
a large spoonful of gin jam
Fill a shaker with ice and add ingredients, strain over crushed ice
   and garnish with second spoon of jam and a raspberry. Serve in an
   old jam jar (I would anyway)

Again, the scope for at-home experimentation is clear and no one will
give you an odd look if you load up your shopping trolley with a variety
of tasty preserves. The Gin 'n' Jam principle would work equally well
with Dockyard's Strawberry, Tanqueray's Blackcurrant or any number
of alternatives.

Gimlet

Back to the classics, but continuing the citrus theme, we come to the **Gimlet**. In his novel *The Long Goodbye* Raymond Chandler has one of his characters confidently asserting that 'a real gimlet is half gin and half Rose's lime juice cordial and nothing else'. That was in 1953, though, and today might be thought somewhat on the sweet side, so you could cut the amount of cordial you add or substitute freshly squeezed lemon juice and simple syrup to taste.

Or, remembering where Rose's was first produced, keep the Leith connection going (it's the port next to Edinburgh, traditionally home to any number of drinks companies and Rose's original base) but bring the drink bang up to date by using the superbly packaged and very, very tasty Lind & Lime Gin from the Port of Leith Distillery. They suggest mixing one part freshly squeezed lime juice with two parts Lind & Lime Gin and sugar syrup to sweeten to taste. It might help to get outside a couple before your next trip to Easter Road to watch Hibs pull off their usual 'flatter to deceive' act. So let's go with

> 50ml Lind & Lime gin
> 25ml fresh lime juice
> sugar syrup to taste

English Garden

Lightening the mood might be achieved with the **English Garden** cocktail. It's a lovely, light drink ideal for sipping in the spring sunshine. No one seems to know who invented this, or where it came from, or even when. Suddenly, though, it appeared and our lives are all the better for it.

The quintessentially English Cotswolds gin seems the right base for this. Their regular Cotswolds Dry would be excellent here, but for a twist, try their Wildflower gin. There are two variants – the imaginatively named Number 2 includes elderflower as a botanical so might be a logical choice. Their recipe involves

> 50ml Cotswolds Dry gin
> 25ml elderflower liqueur
> 12.5ml fresh lime juice

75ml pressed apple juice
Place all ingredients into an ice-filled shaker, shake and strain into
   ice-filled copa glass

Cotswolds explain that due to the large volume of botanicals used, the gin may appear hazy when ice or tonic is added. That's not a cause for alarm, but if you don't care for the appearance in the gin itself, using a cloudy apple juice will make a feature of the billowing pearlescence that will now appear in your glass. Regarding the elderflower liqueur, try St Germain; worth it for the gorgeous bottle alone.

They suggest garnishing with cucumber, mint and viola flower. Personally, I'd leave the flower in the garden where it looks pretty but the mention of cucumber does remind me that some people make the **English Garden** with cucumber-led gins, such as Cucumber (pp. 72–73) or Hendrick's (pp. 102–03). Dr Samuel Johnson, on the other hand, remarked to his friend James Boswell that 'It has been a common saying of physicians in England, that a cucumber should be well sliced, and dressed with pepper and vinegar, and then thrown out, as good for nothing'.

It appears though that he may have recycled that remark from a curiously similar quip by the Bishop of Peterborough to the Earl of Nottingham in 1689, nearly a hundred years prior to the two friends' famous tour of the Hebrides. Despite spending a great part of his life in London during the height of the original Gin Craze, Johnson is not recorded as offering any wit or wisdom on gin (though he did, on occasion, mention whisky and once famously suggested that 'brandy will do soonest for a man what drinking can do for him' though, being abstemious in his consumption of alcohol, hardly intended this as a recommendation). Perhaps if he had only ventured to try a little gin, he might have found a use for cucumber; certainly, much London gin of his period would have benefited from the addition, or more probably should have been thrown out as good for nothing and quite likely injurious to health.

French 75

I was going to include the Ramos Gin Fizz as it's an absolute classic, but done properly it requires the Old Tom style of gin, egg white, cream and orange flower water – ingredients which won't be found in every home. If this brief mention has piqued your curiosity, there are a number of recipes on the web. For something simpler I suggest the **French 75**. Created in 1915 at Harry's New York Bar in Paris, the cocktail was reputed to pack a punch reminiscent of being shelled by the French 75mm field gun. War, huh, yeah. What is it good for? Well, now we know: gin-soaked champagne.

50ml London Dry gin
30ml freshly squeezed lemon juice
15ml sugar syrup
75ml champagne
Shake over ice and pour into a champagne flute. Once settled,
    pour champagne gently down a spoon allowing it to sit on top
    of the gin mix. Some recipes add powdered sugar to the lemon
    juice. You can, should you choose, drop in a sugar cube though
    I wouldn't bother. Garnish with lemon

The champagne matters. Bollinger for preference, though I find the Krug Grande Cuvée 168ème Édition is quite agreeable. Sorry, just kidding: some decent prosecco or cava will work fine here. If you prefer a sweeter taste but don't want to add the sugar lump then check the label for demi-sec (prosecco) or seco or semi-seco (cava), though somewhat harder to find. Once you've opened the bottle of fizz, you'll soon find willing helpers to empty it (stoppers are available).

Martini

Let's end this brief review with the **Martini**, *primus inter pares* amongst cocktails and beloved of mixologists the world over.

But where to start with possibly the most famous, most keenly debated, most versatile and most written about mother of all cocktails, a beguilingly simple mix of gin and dry vermouth.

Its origins are shrouded in mystery. Some would have it derived from the Martinez while other commentators credit the Marguerite as the source. It may have taken its name from Martini & Rossi's eponymous vermouth (the brand is now owned by Bacardi, who also produce Noilly Prat, which is better if you ask me). It's clear though, that James Bond got it wrong – 'shaken, not stirred' is an affectation introduced by his creator Ian Fleming, who was something of a snob about drinks and most other things as well.

The key thing to determine is whether your taste runs to 'dry' or 'wet' as that indicates the relative percentage of gin and vermouth – dry means more gin and is consequently higher in alcohol. A 'Churchill', named for the famous prime minister, indicates a martini so dry that, to quote the great man, you simply 'observe the vermouth from across the room'. So, 30ml neat gin then. Or more if you're feeling greedy, in which case lob in an olive or two. Very few calories in those.

Author Ernest Hemingway apparently adhered to a similar regime, recommending 'Montgomery' as the measure: that's 15 parts gin to 1 of vermouth. That would suggest 30ml gin with just 2ml vermouth, always assuming you can find a measure that small!

For my own part, I'm definitely in the 'wet' camp, preferring a more generous proportion of decent vermouth. It makes for a longer drink, for one thing, and it's generally possible to manage a second glass before making a complete fool of yourself. Which is probably where we should leave cocktails.

THE
PERFECT
TONIC

Farming quinine trees in Rwanda.

Gin's Best Friend

Let's talk about tonic. After all, as a well-known premium brand maintains, 'If three quarters of your gin and tonic is the tonic, make sure you use the best.'

Until very recently, though, there was very little choose from: there was Schweppes and a few cheaper ones, not many of which were awfully nice. So, Schweppes it was – but here's a short history because, as we shall see, things are very different today.

You owe two nineteenth-century French scientists a big drink. Back in 1820, Pierre-Joseph Pelletier and Joseph Bienamé Caventou worked out how to extract quinine from the bark of the cinchona tree, which grows in the foothills of the Peruvian Andes. Aware of its wonderful properties in treating malaria, the local natives called it the 'fever tree'. Its bark had been shipped to Europe for centuries, but, aware of its value, the newly independent republics of Peru, Ecuador, Colombia and Bolivia strictly controlled the export of seeds and seedlings. which, in any event, proved hard to grow in other than highly specific conditions. Turns out the fever tree is quite a fussy tree.

But, with their empires expanding fast into tropical regions where their colonists and troops were suffering badly in the unfamiliar, unfavourable climates and dying in considerable numbers, the French and British were desperate to produce larger quantities and control the supply. By 1840, it's said that the British were processing more than 700 tonnes of cinchona bark annually, in India alone, but more was desperately needed. Then, in 1865, the British botanist Charles Ledger succeeded in smuggling some seeds out of Bolivia, which were eventually successfully cultivated in the Dutch colony of Java. The species he 'discovered' (if we're honest, pilfered), was rich in quinine. Once cultivated and renamed *Cinchona ledgeriana*, it went on to dominate the world supply of what was then a valuable and important drug.

However, quinine, so effective in preventing malaria and other tropical fevers, is horribly bitter to the taste. Dissolved in the carbonated water originally pioneered by one Johann Jacob Schweppe, it became a more palatable tonic (as in health-giving – 'wellness' is not such a new idea after all), and with the addition of gin was enthusiastically adopted by the British in India. Hurrah! Trebles all round!

Returning colonials brought the fashion for gin and tonic back home and added some respectability to gin's raffish image. Thus, a classic was born.

Sadly, though, over the years, the amount of quinine was reduced and, for cost reasons, artificial sweeteners were employed. Cane sugar was dropped in favour of saccharine, and, in the USA, high-fructose corn syrup was widely used. Quite apart from the fact that we now know this isn't terribly good for you, it accounts for the fact that, in general, American tonic tastes pretty dreadful to the European palate. Pub operators, particularly the owners of the large national chains, began to favour the convenience and cost-saving (to them) of post-mix dispensers – the hand-held 'gun' which serves a scoosh of the desired sparkling beverage from a selection of syrups which the gun mixes with chilled water. Probably the less said about the syrups, the better.

Think about it: it's the bar equivalent of a restaurant offering curry, pizza, burgers, Chinese *and* fish and chips, all at bargain prices. Do you really want to eat there? Post-mix dispensers may suit the operator and the grey-faced accountants behind the scene, but they're a pretty sure indicator of a bar more concerned with convenience and profit than mixing you the great drink you're hoping for.

With all this going on and changes in drinking fashions that favoured white rum and vodka, gin sales entered a period of slow decline and tonic water followed it into a dark place – but, happily, in recent years this has all changed.

Mostly, this is the work of one brand, Fever-Tree, which was born as recently as 2005 on the back of the boom in crafted spirits. From a small start, it has shaken up the previously rather dull world of tonic waters by using premium, high-quality, naturally sourced ingredients, and, in doing so, it has brought interest and choice back into the category – incidentally causing Schweppes to raise their game with their short-lived 1783 variety and spawning many imitators. Suddenly, everyone is concerned to emphasise the quality of their product and there is a bewildering range of flavours on offer – pomegranate and basil, anyone?

So-called 'craft' tonics, some of them excellent, have popped up everywhere and are almost as prolific as the new wave of gins. These include, but are not limited to – take a deep breath here – 1724, Merchant's Heart, Bermondsey, Buzbee's, Artisan Drinks Co.,

Cambridge, Double Dutch, Tassoni, Lixir, Peter Spanton, Luscombe, Poacher's, East Imperial, Fentimans, Walter Gregor's, Lamb & Watt, Thomas Henry, BTW, The London Essence Company with their distilled essences, and, surprisingly, good old Britvic. I could list many more, but it's becoming tedious and you get the point.

Actually, I suppose the point is that you can find a tonic and a flavour to suit all palates and all gins: you just have to experiment. But it does get confusing and expensive, because the smaller brands may be hard to find and most decent tonics aren't cheap. However, to be completely clear about this, cheap tonic, especially the own-label stuff in large plastic bottles, is a false economy and must be avoided. And, whatever you do, don't put a partially full bottle back in the fridge to use another day.

To help cut through the confusion, the ever-friendly people at Fever-Tree have designed a useful 'pairing wheel' that matches gin styles to the appropriate tonic water. It's reproduced here.

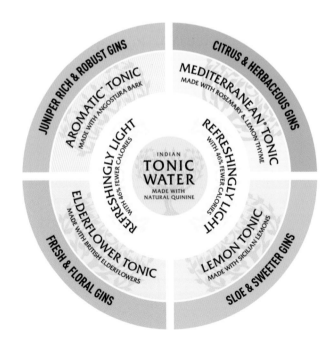

ACKNOWLEDGEMENTS

The biggest thanks go to all the distillers, all around the world, whose energy, enthusiasm and entrepreneurial spirit has made this book possible. And to you for buying, drinking and supporting their products – and for buying this book!

At a personal level, I'd like to thank the long-suffering but ever patient Mrs Buxton for mopping my increasingly fevered brow during the production of yet another book. To be honest, I wasn't sure if I was pushing it, but she's taken up online bridge, so I think I may have got away with it.

The team of Judy Moir (agent), Andrew Simmons (managing editor), Alison Rae (editor) and Teresa Monachino (designer) have done a great job – grateful and fulsome thanks to all of them. And to Abigail Salvesen for the jacket design. Together they have helped more than they know.

To the excellent team at Fever-Tree Drinks, many thanks for the use of photography and the handy pairing wheel, and particularly to Craig Harper and Jaz Arwand for your support and creativity with Buxton's Bucket of Blood and Granny's Ruin.

Finally, please support the distillers large and small, bars and off-licences with your credit cards! Especially now, because they need your money more than ever. And absolutely finally, consider buying another copy of the book for a friend, because I do too. Cheers!

Photography
All bottle pictures come courtesy of the relevant distillery or brand owner and are their copyright property, reproduced here with permission. Other copyright permissions are as follows: inside front and back cover, Bluecoat American Dry Gin; pp. 6–7, Ralf Liebhold, istock; pp. 16–17, Edinburgh Gin; p. 19, Jared Brown; pp. 20–21, Silent Pool Distillery; pp. 202–03, Janet Shepperdson, Alamy; pp. 226–27, Dan Edwards, istock; p. 253, Jaz Arwand; p. 256, Marian Vejcik, istock; p. 260, bhofack 2, istock; p. 263, Maxim Fesenko, istock; p. 264, Sanralise, istock; pp. 266–67, Image Source, Alamy; pp. 268 and 271, Fever-Tree.